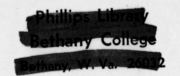

A Garland Series

# THE BALLAD OPERA

A Collection of 171 Original
Texts of Musical Plays
Printed in Photo-Facsimile
in 28 Volumes

Volume XXVI

# SCOTTISH BALLAD OPERAS III

## Farce and Satire

Selected and Arranged by
Walter H. Rubsamen

Garland Publishing, Inc., New York & London

1974

**Library of Congress Cataloging in Publication Data**

Rubsamen, Walter Howard, 1911-1973, comp.
    Scottish ballad operas III.

    (The Ballad opera, v. 26)
    Facsims.
    CONTENTS: Drury, R. The devil of a duke; or,
Trapolin's vagaries; a farcical ballad opera. 1733.--
Thomson, A. The disappointed gallant; or, Buckram in
armour; a new ballad opera. 1738.--MacLaurin, J.  The
philosopher's opera. [1757] [etc.]
    1.  Ballad operas--To 1800--Librettos.  I.  Title.
II.  Series.
ML48.B18 vol. 26      782.8'1'208s [782.8'1'208]
ISBN 0-8240-0925-8              74-8488

*Printed in the United States of America*

# Contents

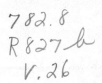

# The Devil of a Duke

*Bibliographical note:*
*This facsimile has been made from a copy in the*
*National Library of Scotland*
*(L.C. 3351.5)*

# THE
# DEVIL of a DUKE:

## OR,

*TRAPOLIN*'s *Vagaries*.

## A

## (Farcical Ballad)

# OPERA.

As Acted at the THEATRES of

*London* and *Edinburgh*.

## EDINBURGH,

Printed: And fold by ALLAN RAMSAY.
## MDCCXXXIII.

# Persons in the Opera.

## MEN.

| | |
|---|---|
| Lavinio, *Duke of* Florence. | Mr. *Peterson.* |
| Brunetto, *Prince of* Savoy. | Mr. *Ware.* |
| Barbarino, } *Lords.* | { Mr. *Miller.* |
| Alberto, } | { Mr. *Fraser.* |
| Mago, *Conjurer.* | Mr. *Bulkelley.* |
| Trapolin, { *a Buffoon* } { *false Duke.* } | Mr. *Wescomb.* |
| Quaker, | Mr. *Price.* |
| Captain, | Mr. *Maxfield.* |

## WOMEN.

| | |
|---|---|
| Isabella, *Dutchess.* | Mrs. *Ware.* |
| Prudentia, *Duke's Sister.* | Mrs. *Woodward.* |
| Flametta, Trapolin's *Sweetheart.* | Mrs. *Miller.* |
| 1. Woman. | Mrs. *Bulkelley.* |
| 2. Woman. | Mrs. *Ayres.* |

SCENE, Florence, *and a Wood adjacent.*

# THE
# *DEVIL of a DUKE :*
# O R,
# TRAPOLIN's Vagaries.

## SCENE I.

### Trapolin *and* Flametta.

*Trap.* FOR ever thine, *Flametta.*

*Flam.* Thanks, my Dear : But am not I a fond Fool to believe you, when I have not seen you these two long Days ? I love you but too well ; for truly, Dear, you are not so good as you ought to be.

AIR I. What shou'd a Lassie do with an old Man ?

*Ah ! shou'd wanton Fancy move you,*
*Shou'd you prove a naughty Man ;*
*I shall think you never lov'd me,*
*I shall hate you, — if I can.*

A 2                                    *Tra*

*Trapolin sings,*

*Shou'd your dearest Beauties move me,*
  *They'd but prove that I'm a Man;*
*You'd then believe I better lov'd you :*
  *Try, —— and hate me if you can.*

Pretty Rogue, how she fires my heart! —— now could
I cry like any roasted Lobster. —— What would old
Lord *Barbarino* give for such one kind Word from her?
—— But young and poor as she is, yet she's constant
and virtuous; —— not that I care much for Virtue nei-
ther.

### AIR II.  *Willy* was a wanton Wag.

*Wou'd you be a Man in Fashion,*
  *And prove wealthy, safe and wise;*
*Indulge yourself in every Passion;*
  *Virtue, Learning, Fame despise;*
*Be rapacious, bold and florid :*
  *Gold alone is the great Prize*
*That takes from Vices all that's horrid,*
  *And makes us pass for good and wise.*
*This clears a Reputation tarnish'd,*
  *And it never yet was found*
*That the Gallows e'er was garnish'd*
  *With a hundred thousand Pound.*
*This clears, &c.*

*Flam.* Let me conjure you leave these wicked Cour-
ses. —— You must indeed, or we must never marry; but
I hope you'll be my Convert, and reform.

*Trap.* All in good Time, Love : It becomes me to
see my Betters go before me; when I do mend, I
shall certainly do it to purpose, I am so long about it.
—— In the mean time I give thee leave to be honest,
and I think that's fair. ——

*Enter* Barbarino *and* Officers.
Who's here, my Rival Lord ?

                                        *Barb.*

*Barb.* Here is the Villain with his handsome Wench,
And (what afflicts me more) an honest one.
I have these many Weeks attempted her;
But neither Threats nor Presents can prevail.
She must be virtuous, or her Poverty
Could ne'er withstand the Offers I have made :
Yet were she virtuous, she would ne'er allow
This wicked Pandar so familiar with her;
This sidling Parasite, Buffoon and Beggar.
But on pretence of his Enormities,
I have procur'd this Order from the Duke
For his immediate Banishment from *Florence.*
Most certain'y he bears some Spell about him ;
And when he's once remov'd, I shall succeed.

*Trap.* Again, my Dear. —— *My good Lord Barberino, your Honour's humble Servant.* —— For this free
Promise, Love, I ne'er enough can thank thee. —— *Your
Lordship's to Command.* —— No Fortune shall divide or
change our Wills. —— *Your Honour's humble Slave.* ——
What's Wealth or Power, where Hearts consent like
ours? —— *Your Lordship's Vassal.* —— When thou dost
sigh, thy *Trapolin* shall weep. —— *Your Honour always
shall command me.* —— And when thou sing'st——

*Flam.* We are observ'd.
Learn to be honest, and I'm thine for ever. [*Exit.*

*Trap.* I beg your Lordship's Pardon. Your Lordship
saw how I was employed. The poor Wretch has taken a Fancy to me; and your Lordship knows I am a
Person of liberal Education; that I bear not a Breast
of Flint, nor was nurs'd with the Milk of *Hircanian*
Bulls. Now if your Lordship has any thing to command me, here I stand ready, I'll *fido Trappalino,* your
Honour's humble Servant in all things possible and impossible.

*Barb.* You are a saucy peremptory Villain,
And have too long escap'd the Stroak of justice.

*Off* Nor is there such a Coward in all *Tuscany*;
He's able to corrupt an Army.

*Trap.* Fear not that *seignior Capitano* ; for I never mean to come into one.

*Barb.* So lewd a Pandar ne'er infected City : What Wife or Daughter of the noblest Blood Is safe, where such a hellish Factor breathes ?

*Trap.* And can your Lordship on your Honour tax me for want of Diligence in my Vocation?

*Barb.* Industrious hast thou been in Villany ; But *Florence* must no longer be the Scene. This is your Warrant, Captain, from the Duke, To drive this Miscreant from our City-gates : And when he's seen again in *Tuscany*, That Minute forfeits his abandon'd Life. Thus has our Duke decreed,

*Trap.* At whose Request ?

*Barb.* On mine.

*Trap.* I am glad to find your Honour has so much Interest in his Highness, and therefore make choice of your Honour as the most proper Person to sollicit my Repeal.

*Barb.* Audacious Slave !

*Trap.* His Highness knows Travelling is chargeable, and besides my Stomach is of no ordinary Dimensions.

*Barb.* Away with him : If he dispute your Orders, Call for the Parish-whips to your Assistance.

*Trap. Seignior Officer*, you may take his Lordship's Word when he says a thing. You hear his Lordship hath private Business with me, and desires your Absence. —— For certain then his Highness is upon Treaty of Marriage withe the *Milaness*. Your Lordship and I were always of opinion it would come to that.

*Barb.* Such harden'd Impudence was never seen. Take him away.

*Trap.* My Lord, my Lord. —— Such a Primrose in a Corner for your Lordship, never blown upon, my Lord; ——

AIR

AIR III. The Lads of *Dunse.*
*Complying, denying,*
*Now free, and now coy,*
*Alluring and curing*
*Love's Pain with its Joy,*
*With Frowns and with smiles, that kindle a Fire,*
*Is a Lass that each Temper and Age must admire.*
*Her Eye darts its Glances,*
*Our Hearts feel the Ray ;*
*Her Power advances*
*As ours ebbs away.*
*From Engagements so strong there's none can retreat ;*
*For do what she will, she's every way sweet.*

*Barb.* Force him along.
*Trap. Flametta,* my Lord ; what says your Lordship to *Flametta ?* There's Eyes and Bubbies! Shall
I bring her to your Lordship ? — Nay my Lord, my
Lord.                              [*They bear him off.*
                                   [*Exeunt.*

*Enter Duke* Lavinio, Alberto, Guards *and* Attendants.

*Lav.* I'm stung with Adders, and shall go distracted ;
Let me have Breathing-room.
*Alb.* Your Highness knows
I ever have been watchful for your Honour ;
And next to that I would preserve your Quiet.
*Lav.* Choice Method! first blow Poison in my Ears,
And after that preach Patience to me.
*Alb.* I fear my Duty has been too officious :
Dread Sir, reflect, where was the mighty Harm
In holding talk with him by open Day ?
I hope this Fanning will incense the Flame.   [*Aside.*
*Lav.* What Harm ? The very Bawd to their Desires
Could never have a Forehead to dispute the Harm.
A Virgin and a Princess seen to walk
And hold Discourse apart with one of Race
                                   Obscure,

Obscure, at least unknown, and no Harm in't?
'Twere lewd, though they had only pray'd together.

AIR IV.   Almanfor.

> *A buxome young Daughter*
> *Makes many Mouths water,*
> *And the Fops all around her will spark it ;*
> *They say they're a Treafure : ——*
> *But gives us no Pleafure*
> *Until they are brought to fair Market.*
>
> *While our Cafh is in Chefl,*
> *We are never at reft ;*
> *For Robbers are rank in this loofe Age :*
> *Our Girls and our Purfes*
> *Are nothing but Curfes*
> *Till they both are put out to good Ufage.*

Bring the audacious Traitor to our Prefence.

[Brunetto *brought in here.*

*Enter* Brunetto.

**Brun.** Dread Sir, and twice my noble Conqueror;

[*Kneeling.*

First in the Field, in which your felf alone
Could ftop my Conqueft with refiftlefs Might ;
And fince in gen'rous princely Favours.

**Lav.** Rife.
I am not us'd to hearken after Praife,
Or Thanks for Benefits by me conferr'd ;
For hitherto they always fell on Merit,
Which can at beft be call'd but paying Debts.
Only in this Acknowledgment, I hear
Ingratitude from its own Mouth condemn'd.
This Lord, the watchful *Argus* of my Honour,
Has charg'd you with a Crime will ftain the Worth
You fhew'd in Battle, and make Valour blufh.

**Alb.** I but inform'd your Highnefs what I faw.

**Brun.** He's prejudic'd : I kill'd his Son in fight,

Iu

In Service of my Prince, as he of you.

*Liv.* I have a Sister, dear to me as Fame,
Our Royal Father's only Care and Comfort:
' My Dukedom (said he dying) I bequeath thee,
' A slender Present, and thy Due by Birth;
' But with it all the Glory of our Race;
' The spotless Honour of the *Medices*:
' Preserve the princely Blood from base-born Taint;
' But most secure it in the weaker Part,
' And match *Prudentia* with her Peer in Birth;
' So shall I with my Ancestors have rest.'
Now Sit, how far you have infring'd these Orders,
And brought a Guilt unknown upon my Head,
I leave your self to judge: Confess your Crime,
And Torture shall revenge it; smother it,
And Tortures shall extort it.

  *Brun.* My charmed Soul
Came panting to my Lips to meet your Charge,
And beg Forgiveness for its high Presumption.
But since you talk of Tortures, I disdain
The servile Threats, and dare your utmost Rage.
I love the Princess, and have urg'd my Passion;
Tho', I confess, all hopeless of Return.
This with a Soldier's Freedom I avouch,
Who scorns to lodge that Thought he dares not own:
Now Sir, inflict what Punishment you please;
But let me warn you, that your Vengeance reach
My Head, or neither of us can have Rest.

### AIR V. O'er Boggy.

*The Dog his Bit will often quit,*
  *A Battle to eschew;*
*The Cock his Corn will leave in Barn,*
  *Another Cock in view:*
*One Man will eat another's Meat,*
  *And no Contention's seen;*
*For all agree 'tis good to be,*
  *Tho' hungry, in a whole Skin.*

*But*

*But should each Spy, his Mistris by,*
  *One contradict his Suit,*
*He quits all Fears, and by the Ears*
  *They fall together to't.*
*Such Rivals shock Men, Dogs and Cocks,*
  *And makes the Gentle froward ;*
*He who won't fight for Mistris bright*
  *Is something worse than Coward.*

*Lav.* Chains, Straw and Darkness! this is meer Dif-
traction!
To Prison with him ; you that waited on him
                    [*They lead off* Brunetto.
Be now his Guard : Thin Diet and no Light ;
Such Usage may restore him. —— Vengeance thus
Converts to Charity.

                    *Enter* Prudentia.

*Prudentia,*
Your Entrance has prevented me a Visit
To your Apartment, and half sav'd a Chiding :
Yet I must tell you, you have been to blame :
But, Sister, learn Reserv'dness for the future,
Such as becomes your Quality ; and hold
That Place which Nature and unspotted Virtue
Has hitherto secur'd you in my Heart.

  *Prud.* Most gracious Sir, if e'er my secret Soul
Admits one Thought that is not first submitted
For Approbation to your Royal Will,
The Curse of Disobedience fall upon me :
As I in you have found a Father's Love,
I shall repay't with more than filial Duty.

  *Lav.* Virtue and Honour ever guide thy Way.

### AIR VI. *Colin's* Complaint.

*As the Bark, when it parts from the Shore,*
  *Has scarce any Distance between ;*
*Yet at last by the Billows 'tis bore*
  *Where, alas! no more Land's to be seen :*

                                        *So*

*So from Virtue when once we remove,*
*We attempt to return but in vain;*
*By the Current of Vice we are drove,*
*Till we founder at length in the Main.*

Thou'rt solitary, but shall quickly enjoy
A sweet Companion in our Royal Bride.
*Sforza* the Duke of *Milan,* our old Friend,
Who always in our Wars hath sent us Aid,
Here offers me the beauteous *Isabella,*
His Daughter, for my Wife; and instantly
We will to *Milan* on the Expedition:
That Treatment once determin'd, we'll return
To *Florence,* where we'll celebrate our Nuptials
With what Magnificence becomes our State.
  *Prud.* Go and be happy, Sir, in your fair Choice.
  *Barb.* That Blessing's only wanting to our State.
  *Lav.* Lord *Barberino* and *Alberto,* you
Whom I have always found most faithful to me,
To you I do commit the Government
Of *Tuscany* till my Return; your Power
  have unlimited: Keep open Ear
To just Complaints; allow and act no wrong;
Look closely to your Prisoner *Brunetto.*
  *Alb.* So may your wish'd Return be safe and speedy.
  *Lav.* Sister, your Tears afflict us; a few Weeks
Shall grace our Court with the fair *Milanese.*
Lead on, 'tis time we were upon our Way. [*Exeunt.*

# SCENE II. *A Desart.*

### Trapolin *and* Flametta.

*Trap.* IS the Wench mad, I say? Wounds! get you
home, you Gipsey: Why I have neither Meat
nor Money, and how the devil do you think I must
maintain you?
  *Flam.* I will go with you to the World's End; I'll
live

live with you, ſtarve with you, die with you.

*Trap.* And lie with me, I ſuppoſe. Why the Fierce-neſs of my Appetite one way, has blunted the Edge of the other: I'm a baniſh'd Man, am I not? 'Tis High Treaſon for me to return to *Florence.* Why, by the ſame Reaſon it muſt be High Treaſon for you to keep out of it.

*Flam.* I did not care what came of me, if it was not for your ſweet ſake.

*Trap.* And is it poſſible you can love me ſo much?

### AIR VII.   Se Gaucci.

*Flam.* *Do not ask me if I love you;*
   *A Maid ſhould anſwer, No:*
*Tho' none I prize above you,*
   *Still I muſt anſwer, No.*
*Thus baſhful Virgins flying,*
   *The wiſh'd for Bliſs forgo;*
*Tho' their Eyes confeſs them lying,*
   *Still they muſt anſwer, No.*

The Duke is gone to *Milan,* and has left *Barberino* and *Alberto* Deputies of *Florence.* Alas! if I return, *Barberino* may oblige me to any thing.

*Trap.* Why, ay, as you ſay, the old Fellow is a little fond of thee, or honeſt *Trapolin* had never found it Death by the Law, to take the Air in his own Country. But your Virtue ſhall be my Shield, and if he has Re-courſe to *vi & armis,* you know what you have to do when the Duke returns. I have ſeen as honeſt an old Fellow as his Deputyſhip, make a pitiful Figure before a religious Jury, when try'd for a Rape.

*Flam.* Ay, but ſuppoſe my Virtue would not be a-ble to hold out againſt ſo ſtrong a Temptation? Ca-pitulation has been the Fate of many a fine Town, when in want of neceſſary Supplies; and if we once come to Terms, you know very well they'll be hard on my Side.

AIR

AIR VIII. In the pleasant Month of *May.*

*Will the Linnet fly the Snare,*
 *When tempted by a pleasing Bait,*
*And the Voice enchants her Ear*
 *Of her long-lost warbling Mate?*
  *Will the Woman e'er despise*
  *The Sight which charms her Eyes,*
  *And be so far unwise,*
*To cast away Gold, her Virtue to hold?*
  *If such a thing is done,*
  *The Fair who can't be won,*
*May surely retrieve all we lost by Dame Eve,*
 *And at Court may die a Nun!*

*Trap.* Return to *Florence,* I say; intercede for my Return with my very good back Friend, Lord *Barberino.* If you can't do without it, promise him what you never mean to perform: He's a Statesman, you know, and that will but be paying him in his own Coin.

*Flam.* Well, I will go then.

*Trap.* But be sure to remember *Trapolin.*

*Flam.* If ever I forget you, may I be sacrificed to the Arms of the Man I hate.

*Trap.* Give me a Kiss, you Gipsey, for that kind Word.

   AIR IX. Birth of *Harlequin.*
    *Will Resolution never*
     *waver?*
*Flam.*  *Fixt as our Fate, I'm ever*
     *thine.*
*Trap.*  *Absence will raise the Fire*
     *higher.*
*Flam.*  *Your ardent Love shall admire*
     *mine.*

     B      *Ev'ry*

Ev'ry long Day,
When I'm away,
Will appear as a Year,
My Dear.        Da Capo.
                [*Exit* Fiametta.

*Trap.* What an inhumane Duke was this, to banish
me, who never banished him! —— Methinks this is a
very melancholy Place; let me think where to betake
myself: I would go to *Rome,* and turn Fryar, but that
I have too much Learning. A Man of my Occupation might once have finger'd the *Pollux Ryals* in *Venice;*
but now the Gentry go a more compendious way to
work, and pimp for one another.—— It quite spoils
all Trading.

### AIR X. To the Hundreds of *Drury* I write.

*Young Damsels were formerly won
    By a Pimp's Application to Mother;
But the Quality saving are grown,
    One does the good Office for t'other.
At Ombre, Basset, or Quadrille,
    They care not Money they squander;
Yet though they disgorge the old Pill,
    They grumble at paying the Pander.*
                [*Musick in the Air.*

Heyday! what have we here? is the Place haunted?
Ay, it must be so; and the good-natur'd Devils are
willing to bear me a Chorus. [*Thunder.*] So, now
the Fiddlers have fall'n out among themselves. Ah,
Lord!—— what's here? a decrepit old Man?

### Enter Mago.

*Mag.* Son, thou art banish'd.
*Trap.* True, old Friend, I am so; —— but how the
devil came you to know it?
*Mag.* The Devil told me.
                        *Trap.*

*Trap.* The Devil he did? —— Why it was e'en his own doing, and so he could give the best Account of it.

*Mag.* Be not dismay'd; Preferment waits upon thee. I am so far from hurting thee, that from poor *Trapolin* I'll make thee a Prince.

*Trap.* Look ye there agen! he knows my Name too; for certain this must be the Devil's Kinsman —— A Prince! poor *Trapolin* thanks you, Father Conjurer, but has no mind to domineer in Hell; I know where your Territories lie.

*Mag.* Besotted Wretch! thou dost not understand me. I tell thee, Son, thou shalt return to *Florence.*

*Trap.* And be hang'd there for my labour.

*Mag.* Be honour'd there, exalted o'er thy Fellows.

*Trap.* On a Gibbet.

*Mag.* There thou shalt shine in Wealth, and roll in Plenty; the Treasures of the *East* shall court thy Wearing, and crowding Beauties sue for thy Embraces.

*Trap.* Sure I must have pimp'd for this old Fellow formerly. Well, as you say, Father Conjurer, (on some private Reasons that I have) this may not do amiss: But how shall it be done?

*Mag.* By *Eo, Meo,* and *Areo.*

*Trap.* What they mean, I know not; but I am satisfied 'tis but going to the Devil for it: And so much for that matter.

*Mag.* Here, sit you in this Chair, and see the Wonders of my Art. *Eo, Meo,* and *Areo,* arise.

*Trap.* What will become of this temporal Body of mine? I am glew'd to my Seat here. —— But here me, good Father, must this diabolical Retinue of yours needs appear?

*Mag.* Of indispensible Necessity.

*Trap.* Then, good Father, let them appear invisible; I have no great Inclination to their Company: to tell you the Truth, I like yours none of the best; you're like the Devil enough to serve my turn. —— Oh, Lord!

[*sinks.*<br>*Mag.*

B 2

*Mag.* Now by the most prevailing Spell
That e'er amaz'd the Powers of Hell,
That midnight Witches ever try'd,
When *Cynthia* did the Crescent hide;
While watchful Dogs to bark forbore,
The Wolf to howl, the Sea to roar :
While *Robin* does his Midnight Chare,
And Plowmen sweat beneath the Mare :
By all the Terrors of my Skill,
I charge you execute my Will.
Now, proud *Lavinio*, little dost thou know
This secret Practice of my just Revenge.

   [*Thunder,* Trapolin *rises drest like the Duke, with
    Devils.*

  *Trap.* Oh Father! what Metal do you take me to
be made of? I am not used to travel under Ground :
Oh for a Dram of the Bottle, of a Quart or two. Call
you this Preferment? Marry, he deserves it that goes
to the Devil for't. —— But I see no Preferment neither.

  *Mag.* Thou dost not know thyself: look in that Mir-
rour.                        [*shews a Glass.*

  *Trap.* Who's there? the Duke? Your Highness is
well return'd : Your faithful Servant *Trapolin* begs of
your Grace to call him home, and hang up this old Wi-
zard; he'll conjure you out of your Wits else, and your
People out of your Dominions. What's he gone a-
gain? he's for his Frisque under Ground too. —— I
have made way for him, I have work'd like any Mole,
and made Holes you may thrust Churches through.

  *Mag.* What in the Glass thou saw'st, is but thy Picture.

  *Trap.* If that be my Picture, I am the Picture of
the Duke.

  *Mag.* And shalt be taken for the Duke himself;
As thou didst here seem to thyself,
So shalt thou to the World appear the perfect Duke.
To *Florence* then, and take thy State upon thee.

  *Trap.* Trust me for Duking it. I long to be at it.
                               —— I

—— I know not why every Man should not be a Duke
in his turn.   Father Conjurer, Time is precious with
us great Persons, and so farewell.

*Mag.* Stay Son, take this enchanted Power with thee;
Preserve it carefully, for at thy greatest need
'Twill give thee Aid : When any Foe assaults thee,
Cast but this magick Powder in his Face,
And thou shalt see most wonderful Effects.

*Trap.* Good! now I am satisfied I am the Duke,
which some shall rue. —— Good Father, fare you well.
—— *Lo, Meo,* and *Areo,* stick close.

AIR XI.  In a Bank of Flowers, *&c.*

*Since the Business of a State's too large*
    *For any Man alone,*
*From others Care I take the Charge,*
    *To lay it on my own.*
*Then how I'll work the servile Rout,*
*New Fav'rites make, turn old ones out,*
    *dal, la, la.*
*Thus the World is wheel'd about.*          [Exit.

AIR XII.  What tho' they call me Country Lass.

*Trap. Now that I'm Duke, I'll strut right high :*
*Come, Courtiers, flatter, fawn and lie :*
*What are the greatest more than I,*
    *But a Stand by, clear the way.*
*And since so kindly is my Fate,*
*With this new Face I'll put on State ;*
*And some shall fall as I grow great :*
    *I pant to see the Day.*

## SCENE III.  *The Palace.*

*Enter* Barberino *and* Flametta.

*Flam.* I Do beseech your Honour repeal my only Joy,
my banish'd *Trapolin* ; take pity on a help-

B 3                                     less

less Virgin's Tears, abandon'd to Distress. You must,
— you will; — for as our Sovereign left his Power
with you, he left his Mercies too.

*Barb.* Indeed, my pretty one, you wrong your Charms.
Nay, I must say you wrong your Virtue too,
By this Concern for an abandon'd Slave,
Devoted to all Crimes: Forget, and scorn him.

*Flam.* I gave my Heart before I knew his Vices,
But it will be my Triumph to reclaim him.
You indeed, Sir, may think the Man unworthy of a
Woman's Love; but, to be sure, the Woman in Love
will be of a contrary Opinion. Besides, Sir, you're
his Rival; and tho' by prejudicing him, you may hope
to profit yourself, I have a Maxim will stop all further Pretensions.

AIR XIII. Buff Coat.

*When once the fond Maid*
*Has Man in her Head,*
*In spite of all Reason she'll love him;*
*And till she has got*
*Your Worship knows what,*
*The Devil can never remove him.*

*Alack-a-day then,*
*'Tis twenty to ten,*
*The Rogue to be gone will endeavour;*
*But she that for Life*
*Is once made his Wife,*
*May hold her own firmly for ever.*

But, I beseech your Honour call him home.

*Barb.* And what Return may I expect for this?

*Flam.* Goodness has always been its own Reward.
But to convince you that your Courtesy shall not be
wholly thrown away upon me, by Day or Night you
shall command ——

*Barb.* What?

                                        *Flam.*

*Flam.* My Prayers.

*barb.* A very hopeful Recompence truly!
What Statesman ever yet took Prayers for Pay?
Deluded Maid, thou dost not know thy Worth,
This Beauty must not be a Beggar's Prize,
Design'd by Nature for a nobler Sphere.

*Flam.* Are you our Prince, my Lord?

*Barb.* What means that Question?

*Flam.* If you were, the Prince shou'd be deny'd.

*Barb.* Then much more I. Why do I trifle thus?
I am no Prince, yet will not be deny'd.

*Flam.* My Lord *Barberino*, what do you intend?
Heav'n shield me!

### AIR XIV. My Deary, if thou die.

*Pure, as the new fallen Snow appears,*
  *The spotless Virgin's Fame,*
*Unsully'd white her Bosom bears:*
  *As fair her Form and Fame:*
*But when she's soil'd, her Lustre greets*
  *Th' admiring Eye no more;*
*She sinks to Mud, defiles the Streets,*
  *And swells the common Shore.*

Sure you design me no Violence, my Lord.

*Barb.* What I intend is Love. If you refuse, you
make the Rape.

#### Enter Servant.

*Serv.* The Duke, my Lord; his Highness is returned from *Milan*.

*Barb.* Ha? the Duke returned from *Milan!* Thou
art mad.

*Serv.* Just now arriv'd, my Lord, and coming hither.

*Barb.* Here, dispose of her as I commanded thee.

Till I find out the Meaning of this Dream.
Ha! that's his Voice, and here he comes in Person.
Let her go, Slave: —— away, dear Maid, away. [*Exit* Fl.

*Enter*

*Enter* Trapolin, Alberto, Spirits, Attendants.

Great Sir, upon our Knees, we welcome your Return.

*Trap.* And upon our Legs we take it. —— Hem, hem!

*Alb.* Your Highness comes unlook'd for. We did not expect this happy Time so soon by fourteen Days.

*Barb.* So, please your Grace, where is our Dutchess?

*Trap.* Your Dutchess will not come till the Gods know when; for my part I know nothing of the Matter.

*Alb.* What means your Highness?

*Trap.* Our Highness means to take an exact Account of Affairs. I left an honest Fellow here, call'd *Trapolin*; what's become of him?

*Barb.* Your Highness gave me charge to banish him.

*Trap.* Why, there's the very Pillar of our State gone: You took him for a Buffoon; but I found him one of the best Politicians in Christendom. Other Countries will value him; and for ought I know, he's a Prince by this time. *Eo, Meo,* and *Areo,* —— brave Lads still,
——

*Alb.* This is mere Frenzy.

*Trap.* And there's another Friend o' mine, *Brunetto,* where is he?

*Alb.* Dread Sir, your Highness knows, that for his Presumption in courting your Sister, you confin'd him.

*Trap.* Nothing but Lying in this World! I confine him! 'Tis well known I never had a Sister in my Life.

*Barb.* No Sister, Sir!

*Trap.* No, *Jack Sauce,* none that's worth imprisoning a Friend for. —— Honest *Brunetto,* I'll be with thee in the twinkling of a —— *Eo, Meo,* and *Areo,* sit fast, Boys. —— Pass.    [*Exeunt.*

SCENE

## SCENE IV. *A Prison*.

*Brunetto solus.*

AIR XV.  Upbraid me not, capricious Fair.

How *servile is the Sate of Man!*
    *How restless and unfix'd!*
*Ev'n Days, which Revelling began,*
    *With Grief are intermixt :*
*Love's fatal Dart attacks the Breast,*
    *When quiet and serene ;*
*And when harsh Care has dispossest,*
    *The delighting Monarch's Rest,*
        *'Tis Anarchy within.*

    *Unhurt by Fear,*
*The airy warbling Choir,*
    *Taste of Love ;*
    *No Thought of Care*
*Annoys the Brute's Desire*
    *In the Grove.*
*'Tis only Man's unhappy State,*
    *These Miseries to bear ;*
*Conspir'd with some Rival's Hate,*
*Thousand pressing Evils wait,*
        *all wait*
*In dreadful Phantoms near.*

*Enter* Trapolin.

*Trap.* What a difmal Place is here ! I'll have it car-
ried bodily out of my Dukedom.

*Brun.* Great Prince ! ——

*Trap.* He makes a very low Leg ; but I scorn to be
out-done in Courtesy, my best Friend *Brunetto.*

*Brun.* I am aftonifh'd ! Sir, upon my Knees, I con-
gratulate your safe Return.

                                        *Trap.*

*Trap.* And, upon my Knees, I do embrace thee, honest *Brunetto.*

*Brun.* I know not what to think or speak : I do beseech your Highness rise.

*Trap.* Not without thee; —— therefore up, I say. Away with Compliments, I cannot abide them.

*Brun.* You honour me above Expression.

*Trap.* A Fig for Honour! I love thee, Man. Sirrah, Jailor, bring Chairs here presently.

*Brun.* Your Highness ——

*Trap.* Away with Highness, I say away with it; call me *Lavin*, plain *Medices.*

*Brun.* Sure I am awake, this is no Dream.

*Trap.* We will live happily together, i'faith we will. —— Come, Sirrah, what a while have you been bringing these Chairs? I have known a Pimp made a Prince in less Time. —— *Brunetto*, sit thee down, sit down, I say.

*Brun.* I will attend your Highness on my Knees.

*Trap.* Why, I am not thy Father, am I? Sit thee here.

*Brun.* On the right Hand! that must not be.

*Trap.* Why, an' thou wilt have it there, there let it be. —— But hold, I am mistaken, that is on the left Hand, that must not be; dost think I have no Manners?

*Brun.* There is no Remedy, I must obey.

*Trap.* Very well. —— What now? art thou afraid of me? marry, an' thou draw'st back, I'll draw back too; therefore sit still, I say, and let us talk. I prithee, Man, how cam'st thou in this damn'd Dungeon?

*Brun.* Ay, now the Storm comes. Pardon me, dread Sir.

*Trap.* What, on thy Knees again? Dost thou take me for *Mahomet*? As well as I can pardon thee, I do pardon thee, whatever it be.

*Brun.* Your Highness knows, my Crime was in aspiring to your Royal Sister.

*Trap.* Hast married her?

*Brun.*

*Brun.* I befeech your Grace.

*Trap.* Well! an' thou haft not, get her Confent, and here I give you mine. So come along to Dinner.

*Brun.* Your Highnefs fhall command me unto Death.

*Trap.* I fay, thou fhalt have her; and if I had two Sifters, thou fhould'ft have 'em both. Who waits there?

### *Enter* Barberino, Alberto.

Now, my Lords, you fee this Apartment, and you thought fit to have *Brunetto* fhut up here, for making Love to my Sifter.

*Alb.* It was your Highnefs's Judgment and Command.

*Trap.* Jailor, take thefe two coxcombly Lords, and keep 'em under Lock. They're never well, but when they're doing Mifchief.

### AIR XVI. My Dady forbad.

*Trap. Such Hang-dogs of State,*
    *They fwell up fo great,*
*By Pimping, by Flatt'ring and Lying,*
    *That the crafty vile Rooks,*
    *Make a Blind of their Dukes,*
*While their Favours they're felling and buying.*

    *But we'll let them know*
    *We'll not be led fo,*
*As we pleafe we will fmile or we'll frown, Boy;*
    *We Tufcany's Duke*
    *On no Man will look*
*With any one's Eyes but our own, Boy.*

In my Confcience and Soul, here is fuch an Incumbrance of Perplexity, that I proteft — Come along, Friend. —

SCENE

## SCENE V. *The Palace.*

*Re enter* Trapolin.

*Trap.* THis Duke's Life is a glorious one! Did e-
ver Man come to Preferment upon light-
er Terms? I am made a Prince, and Father Conjurer goes to the Devil for't.

*Enter* Flametta.

Who's here? my pretty little Rogue; I wonder, what
makes her at Court?

*Flam.* Here's the Duke alone, whom I so long have
sought for, to petition for the Repeal of my dear *Trapolin.* I beseech your Grace, take pity of a Maid be-
reav'd of all her Joys.

*Trap.* All her Joys, that's me.

*Flam.* I humbly beg, poor banish'd *Trapolin* may
be recall'd.

*Trap.* Dear Honey-suckle, she ev'n makes me weep.

*Flam.* Great Sir, that you have noble Thoughts.

*Trap.* I have so.

*Flam.* The World is Witness, and heart-full of Com-
miseration.

*Trap.* Now will I teaze the poor Fool. — But *Trapolin* is a poor scoundrel, beggarly, pimping Knave, —
and it behoves us to keep our Dominions free from such.

*Flam.* Alas! Sir, he has his Faults, as all Men have;
but no other. My Lord *Barberino* has perswaded me

———————————————

*Trap.* To think no more of him: — I do the same
— Hang him, hang him; if you love him, 'tis so
much Love thrown away.

*Flam.* Alas! Sir, you can't judge.

*Trap.* Not judge! and a Person in power! Gran-
deur gives a Man a true Knowledge of every body's
Business but his own.

AIR

AIR XVII. When my Love the other Day.

*Flam. When fond Love's too fatal Dart,*
*Once has touch'd the Maiden's Heart;*
*Led her easy Soul astray,*
*Reason may in vain essay;*
*And discover,*
*In the Rover,*
*Faults to fright her easy Mind;*
*Love to all those Faults is blind.*

*Trap.* Now, suppose I was to supply his Place?
*Flam.* I hope your Highness will desist from such an
Attempt. Consider, Sir, the Crime in persuading a
Maid to violate her Vows.

AIR XVIII. Dainty Davy.

*Trap. Come, come, my pretty dainty Queen,*
*Cease your sighing,*
*Sobbing, crying.*
*Flam. What can your noble Highness mean?*
*Trap. Come my Dear, and try me,*
*I'll only take a Kiss or two.*
*Flam. Oh bless my Heart! what wou'd you do?*
*Trap. Nothing strange, nor odd, nor new,*
*And sure you won't deny me.*

*Flam.* Let me implore you.
*Trap.* I cannot hold out any longer.——Dost thou
still love this same *Trapolin?*

AIR XIX. Hap me with thy Petticoat.

*Flam. Love's the young Heroe Victory,*
*Love, pamper'd Priests, young Nuns:*
*Do good Men joy in Clemency,*
*And witling in their Puns?*

C                                        D*o*

*Do Poets take Delight in Praise?*
*The Beau in Laces clean?*
*So lov'd I, and will all my Days,*
*My banished* Trapolin.

*Trap.* Trapolin's an honest hearty Cock as any in
Florence; and I do promise you upon the Honour of
a Man, and the Dignity of a Duke, he shall be recall'd.
Some of my roguy Lords talk of hanging him ; but I
do assure you, that if ever they hang him, they shall
hang me; and so set thy Heart at rest.

*Flam.* Heav'n bless your Highness, whose kind In-
dulgence to a simple Maid has eas'd her of the Pangs
which Love and tedious Absence caus'd.          [*Exit.*
[*a confus'd Noise without.*
*Trap.* Heyday! What's here to do?

### Enter Officer.

*Offic.* Dread Sir, this is the Day in which your Highness is wont to hear and determine Causes in your
Chair of State; and accordingly here are several Persons come to your Highness for Justice.

*Trap.* What, Justice before I have din'd? I tell you
it is a dangerous thing. I had like to have been hang'd
once my self, because the Judge was fasting.

### AIR XX. *Winchester* Wedding.

*His Fate the poor pitiful Sinner,*
  *Ought ev'ry Minute to watch;*
*When the Judge is in want of his Dinner,*
  *He hangs up the Men for dispatch.*

*But he that wou'd fain be us'd kind,*
  *And live betwixt Terror and Hope;*
*If he stay till his Lordship has din'd,*
  *May slip his Neck out of the Rope.*

                                              Well,

Well, let 'em enter. Here sits the Government. In the first place, I wou'd have the Court take notice, that in Affairs of State, I think that Words are not to be multiply'd; and if I think so, I thal not do so; and if I do not, no body else must——So that in this Assembly, he that speaks little, will fare better than he that talks much; and he that says nothing, better than both.

*Several Men and Women brought in.*

*1st Wom.* I do beseech your Highness to do me Justice. I have liv'd long with Fame among my Neighbours: My Husband too bore Offices in the Parish, till he was kill'd in fighting for your Highness, and left me but this dear and only Daughter, whom this old Sinner has debauch'd, and spoil'd her Fortune.

*Trap.* Debauch'd! that is to say, lay with her, and got her Maidenhead.

*1st Wom.* Your Highness has a most discerning Judgment.

*Trap.* And how did he do this? lawfully, by the help of a Pimp, or unlawfully, without it.

*1st Wom.* Oh, most unlawfully, Sir, for he has a Wife and a Son of his own Inches.

*Trap.* A Son of his own Inches! Good! then the Decision of this Cause is easy——Do you hear, Woman, we will have that Son debauch'd; you shall get the Son's Maidenhead, and spoil his Fortune.

*1st Wom.* I do beseech your Grace——

*Trap.* No replying after Sentence. Whose Cause is next?

*2d Wom.* Great Duke of *Tuscany*, vouchsafe to hear me. I am a poor and helpless Widow, one that had no Comfort left me but my Child, whom this vile Minion, *Whip*, the Coachman, being drunk, drove over, and left him dead; I do beseech your Highness make my Case your own, and think what sad Distress——

*Trap.* Hold, hold, I will have no flourishing. This Cause requires some half a Minute's Consideration more than the former. *Whip*, you say, being drunk, drove over your Child, and kill'd him: Why, look you, Woman, Drink will make a Coachman a Prince; and *vice versâ*, by the Rule of Proportion, a Prince a Coachman; so that this may be my own Case another time. However, that shall be no Obstruction to Justice; therefore *Whip* shall lie with you, and be suspended from driving, till he has whip'd you up another Child.

*2d Wom.* So please your Grace, this is still worse.

*Trap.* No replying after Sentence: Who's next?

*Quaker.* So please your temporal Authority.

*Trap.* How now, my mortify'd Brother, what carnal Controversy are you engag'd in?

*Quak.* Verily there is nothing carnal in my Cause: I have sustained Violence, much Violence, and must have much Compensation from the Ungodly.

*Trap.* What's your Grievance?

*Quak.* I will pour it forth in the Words of Sincerity.

*Trap.* I care not a Farthing for Sincerity, let me have it in Brevity.

*Quak.* This Person here is by Occupation a Mason or Tyler, as the Language of the World termeth it: Whilst therefore I stood contemplating a new Mansion, that I had prepared unto myself, at the same time that this Person occupy'd his Vocation aloft thereon, or rather shou'd have occupy'd; such was his wicked Negligence, that he fell from the Top of the Building most unconscionably, and bruised my outward Man; even with all his carnal Weight, and almost bruised me unto the death, I being clad in thin Array (through the immoderate Heat of the Season) namely, five Cassocks or Coats, seven Cloaks, and one dozen of quilted Caps.

*Trap.* Believe me, Sirs, a most important Matter! If such Enormities go unpunish'd, what Subject can be safe?——Why, if a perverse Fellow take a Pique against his Neighbour, 'tis but getting eight, or ten, or four-

teen

ten Stories high, and so fall down upon him as he
standd, thinking no Harm, in the Street: I do therefore decree, that this Tyler shall stand below, while
you get upon the Battlements of the House, and fall
down upon him.

*Quak.* This is still most monstrous.

*Trap.* As for petty Causes, let them wait ; for till
great Rogues are regulated, little Fools are not worth
notice. *Eo, Meo,* and *Areo,* close Lads.

## AIR XXI. Gamiorum.

*Since in ev'ry Degree of Men,*
 *Servants follow their Masters,*
*Kirkers-like, what Elders pen,*
 *High Zealots mitred Pastors.*
*Roguery on all attends,*
 *'Twixt Creditors and Debitors ;*
*Hang the Knave that ever mends,*
 *A Day before his Betters.*

         [*Exeunt.*

*Enter* Lavinio, Isabella, Attendants.

*Lav.* My Heart's best Treasure, charming *Isabel,*
You are most welcome to the Court of *Florence* ;
And when I lose the Sense of such a Blessing,
Let me become a tributary Lord,
And hold my Birthright at another's Will.

*Isab.* Dread Sir, I know and prize my Happiness,
Blest doubly in your Fortunes, and your Love.

*Lav.* My Absence from Affairs so long——requires
My close Attendance now for some few Hours;
Then I'll return to settle Love's Account:
Mean while our Princess, and her Train, once more
Shall welcome you to *Florence.*

    [*Exeunt all but* Lavinio *and Guards.*

  *Scene opens, and discovers the Prison.*

The Face of Things seems alter'd since I went;
Some strange fantastick Humour has possest,

    C 3           Ia

In general, the Citizens of *Florence:*
As yet I've met with none but speak
Of Matters done by me before I came.
Call *Barberino* and *Alberto* to me, they'll soon resolve.
[*Barberino and* Alberto *appear thro' the Grates.*
  *Barb.* Most Gracious Sir,
Pray your Subjects, and most faithful Servants.
  *Lav.* Confusion! Are my Eyes and Ears both
    charm'd?
Our Deputies, whom we did leave in Trust
Of our whole Power, confin'd in Goal!
Set them at Liberty, and in my Presence now.
Sure some ill Spirit has possest
My Subjects Minds, when I was gone.
Do you know me?
  *Barb.* The Duke of *Florence,* our most gracious Ma-
    ster.
  *Lav.* Are you not call'd *Barberino,* you *Alberto?*
My prudent, faithful Counsellors, to whom
I left the Government of *Tuscany.*
  *Alb.* We are your loyal Subjects, tho' your Prisoners.
  *Lav.* How came you so?
  *Barb.* Great Sir, yourself well knows,
'Twas only for obeying your Commands.
  *Lav.* Some Frenzy has on the poor Wretches seiz'd!
My good Lords, I do beseech you to collect your
    Wits,
And tell me gently how you came in Prison.
  *Barb.* By the Prosperity of *Tuscany,* your Highness
left us there.
  *Lav.* When did I so?
  *Alb.* The self same time you went in Person thither
to free *Brunetto.*
  *Lav.* 'Sdeath! whom! what *Brunetto?*
  *Barb.* Your Prisoner taken in the *Mantuan* Wars.
  *Lav.* I can sustain no more: Come hither, Captain,
these Lords affirm I put 'em into Prison.

                      *Capt.*

*Capt.* Your Highness did, you saw them left in Cu-
stody that Minute you freed *Brunetto.*

*Lav.* He's in the same Tale.
Tho' they are all alike depriv'd of Sense,
Yet do they all agree in what they say:
But why, good Captain, (I will reason't with you)
Shou'd I desire *Brunetto's* Liberty?
Wou'd it not be Dishonour to our House,
To cast away our Sister, upon one,
We neither yet know whom, or what he is?

*Capt.* Sir, it is certain, I did hear you,
To call *Brunetto* Prince *Horatio,*
The second Son to the Duke of *Savoy.*

*Lav.* Vengeance! my Wonder is so great,
That I want Words wherewith to give it Vent.

*Capt.* Nay more, your Highness gave the Princess
Charge,
That she prepar'd herself; for in two Days,
You'd see her married to the Prince *Horatio.*

*Lav.* Captain, I swear to you, by my Dukedom,
I'd rather send for that *Brunetto's* Head.

*Capt.* I beseech your Highness, let your own Eyes
Convince you of the Truth of what I've said.

*Enter* Brunetto, *and* Prudentia.

*Brun.* Divine *Prudentia!* all thy Sexes Charms in
thee are center'd.

AIR XXII. Yellow-hair'd Laddie.

*Some charm with their Descent, and some with their*
*Face;*
*Some enchant with a manner, and some with a Grace;*
*Some only wish Riches to engage them for Life;*
*Some value nothing but Wit in a Wife:*
*But in my dear Choice all Excellencies shine,*
*And paint her out sprung from a Source that's divine.*
*Exit in, &c.*

Prud.

Prud. *Tho' an Enemy captive I view'd your Desert,*
*Which darted a Conquest on my yielding Heart;*
*And now, without Blushing, I own you my Choice;*
*A Brother consenting gives Cause to rejoice.*
*And since my Heart vanquish'd no longer is mine,*
*Accept on't and cherish't, as I will do thine.*
*And since, &c.*

AIR XXIII.   *Europa* fair.

Brun.           *Long gloomy Night,*
                    *Clouded Delight,*
        *Now Care disperses before the bright Day.*

Prud.           *Pleasures improve*
                    *Passionate Love,*
        *Transport appears in its gaudy Array.*

Brun.           *To thy fond Breast,*
                    *I fly for Rest.*

Prud.           *Now Hope appears,*
                    *To quell our Fears,*
        *Only your Faith my Soul alarms.*

Bru.            *All my Heav'n is in your Arm*

*Lav.* Whirlwinds part 'em.
*Prud.* My Royal Brother!
*Lav.* Damn'd infernal Creature!
*Brun.* I did suspect at first, 'twas his Distraction,
That favour'd my aspiring Hopes.
*Prud.* Wherein, dear Sir, have I deserv'd this Usage?
Was't not your Orders?
*Lav.* I'll spend no Breath upon so vile a thing.
You Sir, my new made Favourite, come near,
And tell me, are you Son to *Savoy*'s Duke?
*Brun.* Your Highness knows, I am his second Son.
*Lav.* I know you are his second Son!
The Frenzy has seiz'd him too;
Then know, Sir, were you *Savoy*'s eldest Son,
My Sister once deserv'd a better Match.
To Prison with the Boaster, till *Savoy* fetch him thence.
*Barb.* This relishes of Reason.

                                            *Alb.*

*Alb.* Heav'n preserve this Temper, and restore the Peace of *Florence.*

### AIR XXIV. Dying Swan.

Brun.  *The Vessel thus by gentle Gales,*
  *When wasted near the Land,*
  *Some adverse Wind soon swells the Sails,*
  *And bears her from the Strand.*

Prud.  *The frighted Crew, with wishing Eyes,*
  *Look back upon the Shore;*
  *Till, with the Surges, Fears arise,*
  *They'll ne'er behold it more.*

Both.  *Till, with,* &c.          [*Exit Brun.*

*Lav.* Come, my Lords, and lend your best Assistance to me.
Sleep shall not close my Eyes, nor Food refresh me,
Till I have search'd this Mischief to the Core.
We'll stop at no Extreams of Blood and Torture.
  Baulk no rough Means, that may our Peace secure;
  Such desperate Ills must have a desperate Cure.
              [*Exeunt.*

### AIR XXV. Love's a Dream of mighty Treasure.

Prud.  *With what vast unequal Measure,*
  *Fortune deals our Bliss and Woe:*
  *Happy some taste only Pleasure;*
  *Others only Sorrows know.*

#### Enter Trapolin.

*Trap.* Who's here? The Princess in Tears? Sister, how dost thou do? Come, I know your Grievance; and, out of my natural Affection, have taken Care for you——You marry the Prince *Horatio* this Night.

*Prud.* A Minute then has chang'd his sullen Humour. Why then, Sir, have you made him a close Prisoner?

*Trap.* A Prisoner say you? Run Guards, and fetch him to our Presence. Do not so abuse yourself, dear Sister,

Sister, to think I wou'd confine my Friend to Prison.

*Prud.* You did it, Sir, this Minute; he's scarce there yet.

*Trap.* Madam Sister, if I did it, it was in my Drink, and certainly I had some politick Reason for't, which I have now forgot——Some more Wine, Slave.

### AIR XXVI. Let's be jovial.

*'Tis Wine that clears the Understanding,*
  *Makes Men learned without Books;*
*It fits the General for commanding,*
  *And gives Sodgers fiercer Looks.*
*With a fal, la, la, &c.*

*'Tis Wine that gives a Life to Lovers,*
  *Heightens Beauties of the Fair;*
*Truth from Falshood it discovers,*
  *Quickens Joys and conquers Care.*
*With a fal, la, la, &c.*

*Wine will set our Souls on Fire,*
  *Fit us for all glorious Things;*
*When rais'd by Bacchus, we aspire*
  *At Flights above the Reach of Kings.*
*With a fal, la, la, &c.*

*Bring in the best of Bottles plenty,*
  *See each Glass a Bumper crown'd;*
*None shall flinch, till they be empty,*
  *And full fifty Toasts gone round.*
*With a fal, la, la, &c.*

### Enter Brunetto.

*Brun.* How soon his Mind is chang'd? the Heav'ns be prais'd!

*Trap.* Dear Prince *Horatio,* an' you do not forgive my locking you in Prison, I shall never be merry again. And so here's to you, dear Prince *Horatio.*

                                          *Brun.*

*Brun.* Upon my Knees I pay my humblest Thanks.

### AIR XXVII. *Bury Fair.*

*The Bird whom Fate oppressing,*
*Had coop'd within a Grate,*
*Once tasting Freedom's Blessing,*
*Flies swiftly to his Mate.*

Prud.  *His tender Consort when alone,*
*Gave way to pensive Grief,*
*At Sight of him (by Pleasure won)*
*Finds quick and sure Relief.*

Brun.  *So fly I to your lovely Arms,*
Prud.  *So I receive you there.*
Both.  *We'll bask where wanton Cupid warms,*
*Since Joy succeeds our Care.*

*Trap.* Come, come, take her along, young Man,
take her along. I know Lovers wou'd be private;
and so agree the rest among yourselves.

[*Exeunt* Brun. Prud.

Barberino *and* Alberto *crossing the Stage.*

Who's yonder, my Lord's Banishers at large again?
Will the Government never be able to drink at quiet
for them? Seize the Traitors there, and carry them to
Prison. And do you hear, Sirrah; it shall be Treason
for any body to let them out.

*Offic.* Unless by Order from your Highness.

*Trap.* Orders from my Highness! I tell you, Rascal,
it shall be Treason to let them out, tho' I command
it myself. Away with them, go.

### Enter Isabella.

What *Bona Roba* have we her own?

*Isa.* My dearest Lord.

*Trap.* For her Dress and Beauty, she may be a Dutchess. Who are you, Madam?

Isa.

*Isa.* Do you not know me, Sir? Am I so alter'd since I came from *Milan?*

*Trap.* Oh! 'tis the Dutchess. You are our Wife, you'll say.

*Isa.* Sir!

*Trap.* I am glad of it, I promise you. Come, kiss me then incontinently.

*Isa.* What mean you, Sir? You are merrily dispos'd.

*Trap.* Madam Dutchess, I am somewhat jovial indeed: I have been drinking freely, and so kiss me agen.

*Isa.* My Lord!

*Trap.* You're a proper handsome Woman, I promise you; and tell me, Madam Dutchess, am not I a proper handsome Fellow?

*Isa.* Sir, do not jest with me, you know you are the Man whom I esteem above the World.

*Trap.* What a winning Look was there too?——To Bed, my Dear, to Bed: I'll but take t'other Flask to put State-Affairs out of my Head, and then——ha, ha——

AIR XXVIII. Come Neighbours now.

*While ploting Statesmen, form dull Schemes*
    *Of War and Peace,*
    *And Stocks increase,*
  *In Brokers golden Dreams:*
*'Tis Love and Wine must fill our Mind:*
*And if we Fortune smiling find,*
    *With open Arms*
    *We meet her Charms,*
*Like any Lass that's kind.*
*Then we'll toss off our Bowls*
    *And away with dull Sorrow;*
*Grasp the kind present Hour,*
    *And trust Fate for to Morrow.*

AIR

AIR XXIX. Come brave Boys let's charge, *&c.*

*None but Fools will think of loving,*
  *Till they're warmly flush'd with Wine;*
*Bacchus first, the Flame approving,*
  *Sure to speed at Beauty's Shrine.*
*Wine expert will prompt Desire,*
  *Such as Woman ne'er can blame;*
*Raises high the glowing Fire,*
  *Yet soon cools the burning Dame.*

[*Exeunt.*

*Enter* Lavinio *and* Captain.

*Lav.* You glorious Planets that do nightly guide
The giddy Ships upon the Ocean's Waves;
If some of your malignant Influences,
Have rais'd this Madness in my Subjects Minds,
Let some of your more gentle Aspects now,
Restore them to their Senses.

[Barberino *and* Alberto *appear in Prison.*
My Lords imprison'd! free 'em instantly.

*Barb.* Most gracious Sovereign, how have we deserv'd,
Thus to be made the Scoff of vulgar Eyes?

*Lav.* I wonder, Lords, that you of all my Subjects
Shou'd thus distract yourselves in your wild Firs:
You run to Prison of your own Accord, and say I sent
  you.

*Alb.* Most Royal Sir, you did command us hither.

*Lav.* I?

*Barb.* Your Highness' self.

*Capt.* So please your Grace, you did agen commit
  'em
That very Hour in which you set 'em free.

*Lav.* I commit 'em! I tell you all with Sorrow,
  you are all mad.
Therefore, in this small Interval of Sense,

D                          Betake

Betake you with one Voice to your Devotion,
And pray the incens'd Gods to be appeas'd,
And keep you from Relapse.

*Both.* Heav'ns bless your Highness.

[*Exeunt.*

### Enter Brunetto, Prudentia.

AIR XXX. Why will *Florella,* whilst I gaze.

*Brun.* *I wonder not that Harms appear,*
    *Where Hearts by Love are sway'd:*
  *Pleasure can never come sincere,*
    *While Power is obey'd.*
  *The sudden Glooms, dark Nights disclose,*
    *Will justle with the Morn;*
  *The Briers sweet, the blushing Rose,*
    *Are guarded by a Thorn.*

### Enter Lavinio.

*Lav.* What do I see? *Brunetto* unconfin'd?
Hell! they kiss, embrace before my Eyes! My Guards
    there!

### Enter Captain *and* Guards.

*Brun.* Ha! he's chang'd agen.
*Prud.* My noble Brother.
*Lav.* Oft! Had'st thou Reason, and shou'd'st offer
    this,
I'd study Tortures for thee——as thou art,
I pity thy Misfortunes——seize your Prisoner;
Next time I see him free, your Head is forfeit.
*Prud.* Wonders on Wonders! I beseech you, Sir,
by all the Bonds of Nature, for what Cause?
*Lav.* It is in vain to answer frantick People.

AIR

AIR XXXI.  Fy gar rub her o'er wi' Strae.

*Sparks unheeded, quickly blazing,*
*Burn the noblest Buildings down;*
*And the Sailors, idly gazing,*
*Leaks neglected, Vessels drown.*

*All promote their own Undoing,*
*Who remiss behold its Rise:*
*Caution is the Check of Ruin,*
*And Distinction of the Wise.*

[*Exit.*
[*Scene draws, and shews* Trapolin *asleep;*
*Flasks of Wine by him.*

*Trap.* What a princely Nap have I taken? But as I remember, I was to have gone to my Dutchess, or dreamt so.  Give me a Bumper.

*Enter* Barberino, Alberto.

My Lords at large agen!
*Barb.* Long live your Highness.
*Trap.* Amen.
*Alb.* And happily.
*Trap.* Amen for that too.——But, my small Friends, how came you hither? I thought you had been under Lock and Key.
*Barb.* Alas, he's relaps'd agen.
*Trap.* Sirrah, Captain, why kept you not these Vermin up till I bid you let 'em out?
*Capt.* So please your Grace, I did.
*Trap.* Will you lye, Rascal, to my princely Face?
[*throws Wine in his Face.*
To kennel with them; walk, my good Lords Banishers, your Honours know the way——along with 'em, trugh, trugh.————Thus far, as I take it, we have kept the Government sober, and in good Order.

[*Exeunt.*

D 2                                    *Enter*

*Enter* Lavinio *hastily, and* Servant.

*Lav.* Call *Barberino* and *Alberto* to me.

*Serv.* From Prison, Sir?

*Lav.* From Prison, Slave; what mean'st thou?

*Serv.* Your Highness but this Minute sent 'em thither, nor will your Officer at my Request release 'em, it was so strict a Charge you gave.

*Lav.* Here, take my Signet for a Token ; bid 'em attend me instantly in my Apartment.        [*Exit* Servant.

It must, it must be so.——Some spiteful Fiend permitted by the Heav'ns, assumes my Shape——and what I do, undoes.   No other Cause remains in Nature for such strange Effects.        [*Exit.*

*Scene changes.*

*Enter* Trapolin, Servant.

*Serv.* Here's your Ring again, Sir.

*Trap.* What Ring?

*Serv.* Your Signet which you sent me with; I have accordingly releas'd the Lords.

*Trap.* Give it me : Now, Slave, commend me to *Brunetto,* and bid him start fair,

*Serv.* From Prison, Sir?

*Trap.* From Prison, say you? Here, take my Signet with you agen, and release him ; and say, I charge him on his Allegiance to go to Bed to the Princess.—— Make all fast without there: I can find the way to her Grace by my self.        [*Exit* Servant.

*Enter* Lavinio.

*Lav.* What do I see? This is the hellish Phantom that has bred all this Confusion in the Court.   What art thou?

*Trap.* I am *Lavinio* Duke of *Tuscany.*

*Lav.*

*Lav.* He f. eaks too, and usurps my Name. I'll try if thou hast Substance——struggle not, I'll have thee flead from thy enchanted Skin.

*Trap.* I say, beware of Treason. Flea off my Skin!

*Both.* Guards! Guards! a Traytor! a Traytor!

*Trap.* There's some of Father Conjurer's Powder for you ; what it will do for me, I know not : But there it is.          [*runs out.*

*Lav.* The Sorcerer has blinded me, stop the Traytor.——Help, Guards, Guards!          [*Exit.*

### *Enter* Flametta.

The indulgent Duke has repeal'd the Banishment of my dear *Trapolin*; Heav'n send that Absence may not have chang'd his Mind, and that he return with a warm Heart to me.

### AIR XXXII.

*Fly, Cupid fly, and give my Lover pain,*
 *For why should he,*
 *From Cares be free,*
*And I your Slave remain?*
 *Then draw your Bow,*
 *And let him know,*
*That you will be obey'd.*
 *For why should I,*
 *Thus wishing lie,*
*And live a simple Maid ?*          [*Exit.*

### *Re-enter* Trapolin.

*Trap.* What will become of me? I never can have the Heart to swagger it out with him——the Guards are coming too. I shall be in a Tertian Ague quickly; the Fit's coming on me already. What an Ass was I, to run thus far on the bare Word of a Conjurer, when, without doubt, it was the Devil spoke within him.

AIR XXXIII.  The old Wife she sent to the Miller
             her Daughter.

*Whoe'er would escape from the Dangers of Evil,*
   *Must manage his Business with Cunning and Care;*
*And never rely on the Quirks of the Devil,*
   *The Word of a Statesman, the Faith of the Fair.*
*Courtiers but promise, to bubble their Friends;*
*Woman is kind, when it works her own Ends.*
         *So slyly,*
         *The wily*
   Old Belzebub *bends :*
      *But at a dead Lift,*
      *They all leave you to shift,*
*Wounds! Pox take the Fool who on either depends.*


Cheer up Heart, O rare Powder! It has done the
Work i'faith, and this won't be my Fate.

           *Enter* Lavinio *in* Trapolin's *Dress.*

   *Lav.* I have thee, and will hold thee, wer't thou
*Proteus.*
   *Trap.* Help, Subjects, help————— your Duke's
assaulted!
           *Enter* Captain, Guards.

   *Capt.* What, *Trapolin* return'd! audacious Slave!
   *Trap.* No, no, *Trapolin* was too honest to assault
his natural Prince.——This is some Villain transform'd
by Magick to his Likeness, and I'll have him flead out
of his enchanted Skin.
   *Lav.* Blood and Vengeance!
   *Trap.* Look to him carefully till you have further
Orders.——Now once more for our Dutchess.
                                    [*Exit.*

   *Lav.* Unhand me, Slaves, I am your Duke, your
Sovereign; that Villain that went out, is a damn'd
Impostor.
                                    *Capt.*

*Capt.* Compose thyself, poor *Trapolin*.
*Lav.* What mean the Slaves by *Trapolin*?

#### Enter Servant.

Sir, Are you come? Where is my Ring?

*Serv.* *Trapolin* come home! and as great a Knave
as ever!——it seems he has heard the Duke sent me
with his Ring, and this impudent Rogue thinks to
get it.

#### Enter Flametta.

*Flam.* I'm overjoy'd, my Dear, you're welcome
home.——I fear'd, alas, I shou'd never see you more.
Indeed, my Dear, you are beholden to me, 'twas I
that won the Duke for your Repeal.

*Lav.* Blood and Fire!

*Flam.* This is unkind to treat me with so much
Coldness after so long an Absence. Have you then
forgot my Truth and Constancy?

*Lav.* Off Strumpet!

*Flam.* Oh faithless Man! Women by me take heed,
You give not Credit to the perjur'd Sex.
Have I all thy long Banishment been true,
Refus'd Lord *Barberino*, and his Gifts;
And am I slighted thus?

AIR XXXIV. I wish my Love were in a Mire.

*Inconstant Youth! Behold a Maid,*
*Whose Virgin-Heart thou hast betray'd:*
*O turn once more, that Face to see,*
*Which frown'd on Lords, to smile on thee.*

*From all the World I turn'd my Sight,*
*On thee to gaze, my chief Delight:*
*Titles and Wealth might others move,*
*But my Ambition was my Love.*

*Exit*

*Enter* Barberino, Alberto.

*Lav.* My Lords, you could not come in better
Season,
For never was your Prince so much distrest.

*Barb.* What means the Vagabond? how came he
home?
I hope the Duke will take care to reward him.

*Lav.* Nay, then Destruction is turn'd loose upon
me.

*Flam.* Alas, he's mad! distracted with his Banishment!

*Enter* Isabella, Prudentia.

*Prud.* All these strange Disorders in the Court, must
needs proceed from some prodigious Cause.

*Lav. Prudentia,* Sister, pity your Brother: Speak
to these mad Subjects, who do not know their Prince.

*Prud.* What Fellow's this?

*Capt.* Off Sirrah!

*Lav.* Is she bewitch'd too? My dear *Isabella,*
Thou sure will own the Duke thy Husband———
Ha!
She turns away in wonder!

*All.* Ha, ha, ha!

*Lav.* Nay, then 'tis time to lay me thus on Earth,
And grow one Piece with it.

[*falls on the Ground.*

*Enter* Brunetto.

*Brun.* Your Highness humble Servant, dear *Pru-
dentia,*
The Duke once more consents to make us happy.
Here is his Royal Signet for our Marriage.

*Enter* Trapolin.

*Trap. Eo, Meo,* and *Areo,* rare Boys still———the
Bed I have found, but no Dutchess; and not one of
her

her Women can tell me where she is —— Why here
they are now all of a Bundle, dear Pig'snye! What a
naughty Trick was this to spirit yourself away, when
you know how frighted I am with lying alone——
My princely Friend, hast thou consummated? No!
that sneaking Look of thine confesses thee guilty.

**AIR XXXV. Greenwood Tree.**

*A Woman like the liquid Tea,*
  *Can yield no true Repast;*
*Till by a Man she sweeten'd be,*
  *And suited to the Taste.*
*Like Coffee sinks the single Dame,*
  *To the Bottom of the Cup,*
*Till Man exciting Cupid's Flame,*
  *Boils Inclination up.*

Well married or not married, I am resolved to see you
a-bed incontinently.

*Lav.* The Devil you shall.

*Flam.* Dear *Trapolin*, be quiet——You'll destroy me
and yourself. I do beseech your Grace, forgive him.
Alas, he's lunatick!

*Trap.* Poor *Trapolin*, that ever such good Parts as
thine shou'd come to this!

*Lav.* I am *Lavinio,* Duke of *Tuscany*.

*Flam.* Nay, prithee *Trapolin*, hold thy Tongue,
don't distract us at this rate.

*Trap.* Shew him the Glass.

*Lav.* What do I see? Ev'n thus I seem to them.
Plagues, Death and Furies, this is Witchcraft all.
Still I assert my Right——I am *Lavinio*.

*Trap.* Nay, then I see, he'll ne'er come to Good.
To Prison with him, take him away.

[*Mago appears in a Storm.*]

*Mag.* Turn thee, *Lavinio*, Duke of *Tuscany*.

*Lav.*

*Lav.* Ha! what art thou, that owns my Power and Title?

*Trap.* Father Conjurer here! I warrant he's going to the Devil now, and calls at Court for Company.

*Mag.* Remember, *Guicardi*, the *Tuscan* Count, Whom twelve Years since, thou didst unjustly banish; Which tedious Hours I chiefly have apply'd To magick Studies; and, in just Revenge, Have rais'd these strange Disorders in thy Court. Now pardon what is past, I'll set all right.

*Lav.* By all the Honours of my State, I will.

*Trap.* So, here's his Grace and the Devil upon Articles of Agreement; and excluding me from the Treaty. Well, I'll e'en banish myself, while I have the Authority in my own Hands.            [*Exit.*

*Mag.* Then take that Chair——
                    [*places the Duke in a Chair.*

*Brun.* What mean these Prodigies?

*Mag.* You Spirits fram'd of milder Elements; You that controul the black malicious Fiends, Be kind once more, and execute my Will.

      [*Spirits rise and dance. Mean while the Duke is transform'd to his own Likeness.*

*All.* The Duke! Good Heav'n! long live your Highness.

*Lav.* Sure, all has been a Dream!

*Mag.* Brave Prince *Horatio*, your eider Brother, the Duke of *Savoy's* dead.

*Lav.* Then he is *Savoy.* Sir, I entreat Forgiveness of what's past, and wish you Joy——            [*gives him* Prudentia.

*Brun.*
*Prud.*   } You crown our Happiness.

      Enter Trapolin *in his own Dress with Spirits.*

*Lav.* Here's the Impostor!

                        *Trap.*

*Trap.* Good Father Conjurer, for old Acquaintance fake, I befeech your Grace, ufe Moderation. You may fee by me, what a Prince may come to.

*Lav.* Thy Pardon's granted; but depart the Realm.

*Flam.* Dear *Trapolin,* embrace the happy Fate, and take me with thee.

*Trap.* My Lord, I have ftood your Lordfhip's Friend.

*Brun.* In *Savoy,* I'll requite thee, *Trapolin.*

*Trap.* *Savoy,* Girl, *Savoy.* A Count, a Count at leaft.

*Flam.* Ay, but fhall I go with you?

*Trap.* Hold, hold, I hope his Grace will give us Leave to celebrate here. If he compels us to be gone before we have confummated———

AIR XXXVI. *Nanfy's to the Green Wood gane.*

*Lav.*  *Now all's reftor'd to rights again,*
  *And Falfhood is difcarded;*
  *Let founding Joy reign o'er the Plain,*
  *And Virtue be rewarded.*
  *When crofs Events in Life appear,*
  *That wrap in Clouds their Meaning,*
  *They give us Pain; but when they clear,*
  *They then are entertaining.*

*Trap.*  *Since I no more a Duke can be,*
  *Adieu to all that's ftately:*
  *Come, Flamie, e'en let thee and me*
  *Strive to live kind and quietly.*
  *If we enjoy Content and Love,*
  *Altho' our Rents be fcanty,*
  *Our real Joys may rife above*
  *The Petts of Pride and Plenty.*

# FINIS.

# A TABLE to the SONGS.

The Disappointed Gallant

# THE
# *Disappointed Gallant*,
### OR,
# BUCKRAM IN ARMOUR.
## A NEW
# BALLAD OPERA.
### As it was Acted at the
## NEW EDINBURGH THEATRE.

---

Written by a YOUNG *Scots* GENTLEMAN.

---

Aut prodesse debent, aut delectare poetæ
Aut simul & jocunda & idonea dicere vitæ.
Quicquid precipies esto brevis —

Hor. de Art. Poet.

---

---

# EDINBURGH,
## Printed in the Year MDCCXXXVIII.

# TO THE
# RIGHT HONOURABLE,
# *JANET*
## Countess of *WEMYSS*.

Madam,

IS exceedingly well known, that the unmerited Applause, which this trifling Work has received, is owing to your Ladyship, and that * Honourable Family, by whose Recommendation it was that your Ladyship was pleased to give it Countenance, without which I never cou'd have had the most distant View of Success; yet altho', by this, I have laid myself under an Obligation, which is not in my Power to repay, I have made bold to sue for a second Favour, I mean, That since I have, with so much Confidence, if not Impudence, dar'd to expose unto the World, a Parcel of undigested Thoughts, the Production of a rude and unexperienced Brain, I hope your Ladyship will indulge

* *The Dalrymples.*

# DEDICATION.

dulge these fond Expectations I have entertained, of being screen'd under the Patronage of one, who, upon every Occasion, has shewn a generous Regard to your native Country, in giving Encouragement to any Thing that had the smallest Glimmering of common Sense, especially if it tended to dispel the affected Gravity and Peevishness of Temper, which all other Countries so justly condemn in ours.

IT were, indeed, to be wished, that those who prat of Religion, and the Practise of Virtue, wou'd vaunt of it less, and exercise it more, since, while they superstitiously observe the outward and ceremonial Part, those Things of smallest Consequence, they overlook, and intirely neglect the weightier Matters of the Law, *to wit*, those God-like and Heaven-born Qualifications of Charity and Mercy. This, MADAM, with a sincere Acknowledgment of your kind Favours, is all from,

MADAM,

*Your Ladyship's*

*most humble and*

*devoted Servant,*

The Author.

# PREFACE.

## TO THE

Ladies and Gentlemen of *Edinburgh*, and all good-natured Readers.

Ladies and Gentlemen,

*S*INCE *the Appearance of this Affair upon the Stage, which (contrary to my Expectation) my good-natur'd Audience was pleased to let away with its Life, I have been much importun'd, by those who were daily harrassing me, either for a Copy of some of the Songs, or a reading of the Play, (which, to grant, wou'd have been an endless Trouble) to publish it.*

*And altho' I cannot exculpate myself from the Imputation of Pride and Vanity, while, at this early Time of my Life, I shall dare to expose to the World any Thing that is the Production of my unpolish'd and home-bred Invention; yet I* **think**

think I am under some Kind of Necessity to give a short and genuine Account of its Origine and Progress. To begin then.

It is well known to my intimate Acquaintances, that I have had the scrawl Copy of this by me for about these five Years bypast, and I never made any Secret of it, but shew'd it to a great many, and even gave them several of the Songs they desir'd; by which, I think, it is evident, that originally it was never design'd for the Stage: But, as all young People are fond of their own Performances, I was easily perswaded (about two Years ago) to shew it to the Players, and ask'd if they wou'd act it? And I was answer'd, If I wou'd get it well recommended, they wou'd: But by the Advice of those who had more Judgment than I had myself, I was advised to keep it until the next Winter, and make some Alterations on it. This I did, and at length expos'd it on the Theatre, where (more from the good Nature and Partiality of the Company, than from any Merit in the Work, or extraordinary Performance in the Players, except Mr. Wescomb) it met with a very kind and favourable Reception.

This being the true State of the Affair, I hope it is easily to be observ'd, that as it

was

# PREFACE.

was well known amongst my Acquaintances, long before I had any Thoughts of introducing it upon the Stage, so it was out of my Power to conceal myself as the Author, e'er I was aware. And let any one say impartially, whether or not his Vanity wou'd have allow'd him to conceal a Thing of this Kind, at fifteen Years of Age. I must frankly own mine wou'd not; yet I have often wish'd, from the Bottom of my Heart, that it had. But then, it will be ask'd, Why (after I was sensible of the Disadvantage I labour'd under, in being known) I insisted upon having it further expos'd upon the Stage?

In Vindication of myself in this Point, I must beg Leave to observe, that there is not one in Being, who wou'd (if he cou'd by any Means prevent it) be generally esteem'd a Fool, or Coxcomb; but this must have been inevitably my Doom, had not the World seen it in a publick Manner, even such as it is; for, as Malice and Detraction always exert themselves with full Vigour upon such Occasions, so, at this Time, there was not wanting a considerable Number who took all Opportunities to condemn it, for Nonsense, and (as I am informed) when some of them have been ask'd, If they had seen it, or knew any
that

*that had, they have anfwer'd, No. Now as a great many had condemned it unfeen, I thought it was impoffible that I could lofe any Thing by letting it be feen.*

*And here I cannot but lament thofe common and prevailing Vices of Envy and Detraction, which, I believe, never more abounded than at this Day. I wou'd advife thofe Gentlemen ferioufly to perufe the 23d* Spectator. *He (having handled that Story much better than I can pretend to) begins that Paper with informing us,* There is nothing more betrays a bafe and ungenerous Spirit, than the giving of fecret Stabs to a Man's Reputation; they are like poifon'd Darts, that fly in the dark, and not only inflict a Wound, but make it incurable, &c. *And near the End he tranfcribes a Fable out of Sir* Roger L'Eftrange, *which, I think, has an admirable Moral, and may juftly be recommended to the Confideration of thofe People who make a Sport of Scandal and Defamation. It is as follows.* A Company of waggifh Boys were watching of Frogs at the Side of a Pond, and ftill as any of them put up their Heads, they'd be pelting them down again. Children, (fays one of the Frogs) you never confider, that tho' this may be Play to you, it is Death to us.

*It*

# PREFACE. ix

*It is in this Way that these malicious Mortals divert themselves at another's Expence; and as it is the Mark of a base and ungenerous Spirit, so it is the continual Attendant of a cowardly Soul, since he thrusts at a Man behind his Back; and altho' his Enemy be never so powerful, yet he is intirely safe, having taken Care to conceal himself, and by these Means the Person defamed finds himself hurt, but by whom he cannot tell; so that he will be in the same Condition with one of Virgil's Heros, Æneid. ix. Lin. 420.*

Sævit atrox Volcens, nec teli conspicit usquam
Auctorem, nec quo se ardens, immittere possit.

*But yet I hope it shall be accounted no just Consequence from what has been said, that none shall be allow'd to have a Freedom of judging, and venting that Judgment in Criticism, when they shall think it reasonable; or that I shou'd imagine there was no Room for it my Performance. I am far from such a Thought; and I shall appeal to my intimate Acquaintances, if they have not several Times convinc'd me of its Imperfections, which wou'd have taken up more Time to amend, than I had to bestow; and therefore I hope the good-natur'd Reader will accept of it*

b

*as*

as it is, and paſs by all its Blemiſhes, as the Folly of Youth; and, to make an A-tonement, in ſome Meaſure, for what I have done, I here promiſe never to trouble the Publick with any Thing of this Kind, until I have had more Experience and Knowledge in the World, being conſcious, that, at preſent, I am no Way proper for ſuch an Undertaking: Yet, if any one thinks he has a particular Turn for Criticiſm, I make him very welcome to exert his Talent upon it; but if he once begins to it regularly, I am afraid it will tire him, he may find ſo much ado.

# PROLOGUE.

## By a FRIEND.

### Spoken by Mr. WESCOMB.

YE awful Judges, who in Council sit,
  To pass the Poet's Sentence in the Pit,
With Brow severely bent, and ruthless Frown,
As if ye were resolved—to knock him down.
Already in your Looks—I read his Fate.
Unhappy Youth—but, ah—'tis now too late
To save him from Destruction; oft I try'd
To break his rash Resolves—Blood, still he cry'd,
Perform the Play—no Fear the Town despise
A first Attempt like this, they'll be more wise
Than frighten others from the Hopes of Bays,
And lose the Jest—of damning future Plays.
No, says he, if they damn it, I ll be hang'd.
Done, says I—and if not, I shall be bang'd:
Nor should I grudge a Drubbing, so 'twou'd free
From Flames the Play, and th' Author from the Tree. }
Judge then, which shall be the Catastrophe.
If you should damn the Play, the Poet's Neck
Must suffer—if you save it, then my Back.
Consider, Hanging is a woful End,
And since you find I am so much a Friend
To th' Author and his Work, that, for their Sakes,
I'd gladly bear some half a dozen Thwacks,
You sure must pity, since you need not lose
One Inch of Skin, nor stand in Fear of Blows;
And yet, alas! methinks I see him swing,
Methinks I hear the House with Hisses ring.
You all begin to damn, each in your Spheres,
As soon as on the Stage one Scene appears.
You barbarous Criticks cry—the Man's a Dunce,
Come, without more, let's damn it all at once.
You mighty Sages, who'd be thought far gone
In Books, cry out—The Humour's not his own.
You gaudy Fops, who flutter there in Throngs,
Have Right to damn whate'er to Dress belongs; }
You Smatterers in Rhyme—condemn the Songs.

And

# PROLOGUE.

*And you, you dreadful Wits, who judge by Rules,*
*And think that all the World besides are Fools,*
*Condemn the Passions, Fables, Manners, Plot,*
*The Morals, Diction, Sentiments, what not.*
*Such is the Fate of Plays, no sooner born,*
*Than thus by cruel Midwife Critick torn.*
*But, O! you lovely Dames, in your bright Eyes,*
*Methinks I see some soft Compassion rise;*
*Your tender Hearts must mourn the Author's Fate,*
*Then shew your Pity ere it is too late.*
*If, when the Play is done, you hiss, he's hang'd,*
*But rather clap, and let my Hide be bang'd.*
*Your gentle Smiles will gain the pretty Fellows,*
*And save the Poet's Collar from the Gallows.*

---

## Dramatis Personæ.

### MEN.

| | |
|---|---|
| *Sir* Robert Careless, | *Mr.* Wrightson. |
| *Mr.* Rover, | *Mr.* Bridges. |
| *Mr.* Andrew Trimmer, | *Mr.* Frazer. |
| Sandy Buckram, | *Mr.* Wescomb. |
| Tom, (Rover's *Servant*) | *Mr.* Millar. |
| Cook, | *Mr.* Duncomb. |
| Butler, } *Serv. to Sir* Rob. | *Mr.* Vaughan. |
| Coachman, | *Mr.* Hamilton. |

### WOMEN.

| | |
|---|---|
| *Lady* Careless, | *Miss* Thomson. |
| Belinda, | *Mrs.* Millar. |
| Heiress, (*a Cocquet*) | *Mrs.* Bridges. |
| Mally, (*Lady* Careless's *Maid*) | *Mrs.* Woodward. |
| **Jean** Buckram, (Sandy's *Wife*) | *Mrs.* Bulkely. |

**SCENE** *in and about* Edinburgh.

# BUCKRAM in ARMOUR.

## A new BALLAD OPERA.

## ACT I.    SCENE I.

*A Taylor's House.  Buckram at Work upon the Table.*

### AIR I.  New Killycrankie.

OF all the Tradesmen in the Town,
    Or in our Corporation,
There's none wou'd live a better Life
    Than I in all the Nation,

**II.**

Was but that Jade out of my Sight,
    Who scolds that none can bear her,
Or if I durst but try a Fight,
    To Pieces I would tear her.

**III.**

To stand up stout, and not to move,
    Ha! Faith, that might molest her,
Why may not I my Courage prove?
    Perhaps I'd then be Master:

**IV.**

If once her saucy Pride were laid,
    No more she'd triumph o'er me,
I'd be, as Victor, then obey'd,
    And make her fly before me.

Yes, yes, I'll do all this, if I dare — Dare, did I say?
Why, who shall hinder me? Am I not Master of my
own House — ay, that I am, and she shall find it so, if
this good Yard stands my Friend, [*rising off the Table*]
Confound all Satan's Brood, say I; I'll be subject to none
of them — 'Tis a very fine Story, indeed, that a Man

A

of my Honour and Courage — Courage! No — I can't
brag much of that — but for Honour — Why, I am a
Taylor; and muſt I condeſcend to keep a Wife, who
ſcolds worſe than any Oyſter-Woman, forſooth, and who
calls me a Thouſand raſcally Names, and ten to one but
each is followed with a broken Head — I'll ſuffer it no
longer; and, as a Proof of my riſing Courage — I'll put
on my Coat, and not ſtitch one Thread more this Day.
[*Puts his Coat half on. A Noiſe within. He ſtarts*] Ha!
what Noiſe is that. [*Liſtning*] It muſt be my Wife —
Ay, Pox take her, ſhe's juſt getting out of her Bed, and will
be here in an Inſtant. Now, all the wiſe Men in the Weſt
inſtruct me what to do — Shall I put off my Coat, [*endeavouring to put it off*] or ſhall I keep it on, [*puts it
on*] No, I muſt put it off, [*puts it off*] but I'd much rather keep it on. [*While in this Struggle, enters* Jean.

*Jean.* Sandy, *Sandy*, Why an't you at Work, you Raſcal? What, is your Brain turned? — Sure the Fellow's
mad! Hey-day, you have got your *Sunday*'s Clothes on,
too!

*Buck.* Faith, my Dear, I thought it had been *Sunday*,
and I was going — why, I was going to Church —
there's no Harm in that, I hope.

*Jean.* To Church — No, you Scoundrel, that was not
the Matter, you was Dreſſing to go to the Ale-Houſe,
and leave your poor Wife and Family.

*Buck.* Wife and Family — that's a good Joke, truly;
we have been but ſix Weeks married, and you talk of a
Wife and Family. Ha, ha, ha. [*laughs.*]

*Jean.* Why, hark ye, *Sandy*, how dare you have the
Impudence to laugh at your Wife? Why, ſure, Sirrah,
you forgot that you're married, but I'll make you remember it, [*pulls out a Whip from under her Apron, and beats
him*] Villain, Raſcal, filthy, naſty, ſcoundrel Dog!

*Buck.* Alo! — What do you mean? — Come, come,
prithee be quiet, *Jeany*, I was but in Jeſt, I did not
think that it wou'd have anger'd you, my Dear.

*Jean.* Learn to Time your Jeſts better, *Sandy*, and
you'll be the better uſed for 'em — but I ſee you have pro-
fited a little by my Inſtructions, and, in a ſhort Time, I
am hopeful you will turn a much better Man, but 'twill
take a little Pains, or ſo.

*Buck.*

*Buck.* Pains! — The Devil take me, if I don't feel your Pains moſt ſeverely. [*Aſide*] But let me beſeech you to lay aſide that ill-natur'd Weapon — I don't like it at all.

*Jean.* No, no, *Sandy*, I muſt not do that, for this will make us Friends, now and then, when nothing elſe will; therefore pray don't inſiſt upon that.

### AIR II. Harliquin Tune.

*Bid the Quack give o'er his Tricks;*
*Can he do't? Will he do t? Sure he will not do't.*
*Think you, then, I'll quite my Stick?*
*I cannot, I will not, I never will do't.*

### II.

*When the Courtier takes no Bribes,*
*And Money's refus'd by a Patriot Lord;*
*When Juſtice o'er each Court preſides,*
*Then I will reſign up my Stick and my Cord.*

*Buck.* Truly, then, I may ſave myſelf the Trouble, for that will never be — Judging every one by myſelf, I think no Man will refuſe Money, be the Conditions what will.

*Jean.* Very true; but are Mr. *Rover*'s Clothes ready yet?

*Buck.* I have been working at them all this Morning, and if you'll give me a hearty Breakfaſt, I'll give them the finiſhing Stroke in Half an Hour.

*Jean.* With all my Heart. Come, give me ſome Money to buy Victuals.

*Buck.* Eh! — Did not I give you Two Shillings yeſterday, to buy Victuals?

*Jean.* Hear you, *Sandy*, I'll give you an Account how I diſpoſed of that, but don't grow ſaucy upon't, for I won't make a Cuſtom of it — Yeſterday, I took a ſevere Cholick, and wou'd have dy'd, if I had not bought a Mutchkin of Zerry to myſelf; and you wou'd not loſe a good Wife for a Shilling, wou'd you?

*Buck.* For the one Half of it, I wou'd ſee her at the Devil. [*Aſide*] But that was but one Shilling, I hope the other remains.

*Jean.* Hold your Peace, you prattling Scoundrel, until have done ſpeaking. [*ſhaking the Whip.*] Do you think,

I,

I, who have been bred up, all my Lifetime, in Gentlemens Families, could drink it without Sugar, Cinnamon, and Nutmeg, having a natural Aversion to all strong Liquors.

*Buck.* Scandalous Slut, my Belly must pay for her Extravagance. [*Aside*] Well, here is Sixpence; this is all I have in the World, go and get me some Meat, and prithee manage it well.

*Jean.* Well, I'll oblige you for once.        [*Exit.*

*Buck.* Why, now she's gone, I wish she may never return again; I'd be content to lose my Sixpence, or rather give it to any Body that would bring her in dead to me; and really my Reasoning seems very just, for she, under a Pretence of instructing me, and doing me Good, may in a short Time be my Death: *Argol*, by the Law of Self-preservation — I wish her defunct.

*Enters* Jean *again.*

*Jean.* O *Sandy*, *Sandy*, I have got one of the cheapest Pennyworths!

*Buck.* What, are the Victuals grown cheap? Then I shall live like a Nobleman.

*Jean.* No, you thick-skull'd Blockhead, that's not it; some Thing better than Victuals.

*Buck.* Better than Victuals! — that's impossible.

*Jean.* Look ye, Man, I have got this fine Ribbon for a Sixpence, and I saw my Lady pay Half a Crown for such another t'other Day.

*Buck.* What! and must I starve, then? for Heaven's Sake get me some Meat; for if I want my Breakfast, I shan't live till Dinner. Pray, *Jeany*, be perswaded to save my Life.

*Jean.* What wou'd you do, then, if I should breakfast you like a Prince.

*Buck.* Why, then, I'll behave like a Prince; for I have a Stomach — like a King; and I'll do my Endeavour afterwards —

*Jean.* To mend your Manners — Well, then, follow me to Breakfast.        [*Exit.*

*Buck.* Ay Faith, with all my Heart, for I have an excellent Hand at the Spoon and the Cup.

*And tho' I do submit to my Wife's Beating,*
*I'll prove myself a Hero — at good Eating.*

SCENE

SCENE II. *Sir* Robert Carelefs's *Houfe.* Lady Carelefs *and* Belinda.

*La. Care.* How is it poffible, Coufin, that a Woman
of any Spirit can bear with fuch Extravagances as I do?
To have a Husband plaguing one, all Day, with Indifference and ill Nature, and, at Night, to go to the Tavern among a Parcel of Rakes, and came Home by three
a-Clock in the Morning ?

*Bel.* Why, really, Coufin, it is a little furprifing, to fee
fo vaft an Alteration in his Behaviour, in fo fhort a Time;
for I think 'tis fcarcely Six Months fince you were married,
and Three of them, you fay, he has been thus indifferent.
Falfe, fickle, inconftant Man ! how have I feen him,
with a Lover's Eye, tranfported, ftand and gaze upon
your Beauty,

> *Then he wou'd fwear your Face was wond'rous fair,*
> *And that his utmoft Wifhes center'd there.*

*La. Care.* Ere I knew him, my Fortune fmiled upon
me, and Life fled from me like a pleafant Dream, till he,
with wicked Arts, and flattering Tongue, cloak'd under the
Pretence of Matrimony, deluded me. When it was firft
propofed, every Body perfuaded me, nay, my Glafs too flat-
tered me, that I had no Occafion to fear the Indifference or
ill Nature of a Husband, if he had any Humanity : But all is
Difappointment ! And fhou'd I recal the bypaft Circum-
ftances of my Life, and compare them with my prefent
miferable Condition, it were enough to turn me into Mad-
nefs. [*Sings.*

AIR III. Wo's my Heart that we fhould funder.
*A pleafant Train of Years had paft,*
  *When with Succefs my Fortune crown'd me,*
*Then there was nothing I cou'd ask,*
  *For Pleafure fcatter'd all around me.*
II.
*Then I thought it wou'd be ftrange,*
  *For any of the human Nature,*
*To renounce the Truth, and change,*
  *On any Caufe, to be a Traitor.*

II. Be

### III.

*Be hush, ye Thoughts that fret my Breast,*
*And, O ye Powers, grant me Protection;*
*Let my troubled Soul find Rest,*
*And free me now from all Reflexion.*

### IV.

*While my restless Fancy rolls*
*Along the Scenes of bypast Action,*
*A pleasing Pain torments my Soul,*
*That sure will turn me to Distraction.*

*Bel.* Well, *Celia,* I do pity you, and, as far as it lies in my Power, will assist you; but since we have both engaged in Friendship, and as my Misfortune in loving that rambling young Fellow, Mr. *Rover,* who laughs at every Thing that relates to Matrimony, is equal to yours, I must expect a Return.

*La. Care.* You may rely upon it. But tell me, *Belinda,* how is it that you are sincere with *him,* and it is the World's Opinion, that he is so with *no Body;* I'll allow the Man to be well-made, but I take you to be a Girl of better Sense, than to take a Conceit of any young Fellow, meerly upon that Account.

*Bel.* I assure you, Madam, whatever the World may say of him, in the Main he has good Sense; and tho' sometimes, to shew his Wit, he, according to the Fashion, may rail against a married Life, yet, in serious Discourse, I have often heard him confess, that it was, for the most Part, for Argument's Sake; and I own you wou'd very justly blame me, if I cou'd give no other Account of my Passion for him, but only because he has a smart Look. I'll frankly own, that any Thing that is spoke by a handsom young Fellow, has a better Chance of being taken Notice of, by our Sex, than if the same Thing came from one not altogether agreeable; but, for my own Part, I think I can justify this, as well as every other Action of my Life, to be perfectly conform to the strictest Rules of Virtue and Reason.

*La. Care.* Hold, hold, *Belinda,* you don't remember that you are desperately in Love, my Dear; I hope you don't pretend to give a Reason for that.

*Bel.* Indeed but I do; and I think there is nothing more easily accounted for, than the sincere and true Passion of

Love

*Love.* But you'll say, Why do I love Mr. *Rover?* Becaufe I think he has good Nature, Generofity, and folid Senfe; and, after a thorow Examination of him, I find him poffeft of thefe Qualifications; I think he fuits my Humour fo well, that I could be happy whole Ages in his Company; I cannot think of another, becaufe I know of none, with whom I could live fo agreeably, and it is for that Reafon I love him——Forgive me, my dear *Celia,* for thefe laft Words always ftick in my Throat.

*La. Care.* You know, my dear Creature, with me you may ufe all Manner of Freedom, but, upon my Word, you feem to be fo far gone in the Paffion, that I can't help telling you, I'm afraid you have ftudied it too much.

*Bel.* I am fenfible of it, but pray excufe me, dear *Celia,* for it is what I cannot help, nay, you muft not only excufe me, but indulge me in hearing a Love-fick Song.

*La. Care.* Poor Creature——Well, with all my Heart.

[*Bel. fings.*

### A I R IV. *Handel's* Minuet.

*Love is fo commanding,*
*There is no withftanding*
*Its powerful Darts, fo full of Smart.*
### II.
*Why doft thou wound me fo,*
*Cupid, thou God of Love,*
*And leave his Heart cold remaining,*
*My Paffion difdaining;*
*O, wilt thou never this Pain remove.*

*La. Care.* Well, Coufin, fince we are both unluckily fituated, What would you think in joining together, in forming fome Kind of Plot, in order to bring Affairs to a better Condition?

*Bel.* You have juft prevented me, and the Goodnefs of the Defign makes me bold to hope for Succefs; and as you was telling me before, you had fome Reafon to believe that Mr. *Rover* had taken a Liking to your Perfon, I can't help thinking, that this, managed well, would contribute greatly to our Defign; and I beg the Favour, that you would allow *Mally,* your Maid, to wait upon me fomething oftner than ordinary, becaufe I know that *Rover's* Servant, *Tom,* and fhe, keep a clofe Correfpondence.

*La.*

*La. Care.* Your Lodging is not far from hence, and, whenever you pleaſe, you may ſend for her. But who do you think I am to receive a Viſit from this Morning?

*Bel.* Troth I can't gueſs.

*La. Care.* From no leſs a Perſon than the Heireſs of *Kingiles;* and Sir *Robert* went out a little While ago, to meet a Couſin of his, who is come to Town this Morning, one Mr. *Andrew Trimmer*, a ſilly half-witted Coxcomb, I fancy Sir *Robert* will bring him with him to Breakfaſt, and I expect, betwixt them two, we ſhall be very well diverted.

*Bel.* It can't happen otherwiſe, if Mr. *Trimmer* be ſuch a One as you ſay he is; and I warrant you the Heireſs will match him; for I don't remember to have ſeen a Girl of a more childiſh Behaviour. I happened to be in a Company t'other Day, where ſhe fell into Diſcourſe with a very pretty young Fellow; and tho' I did not perceive he made the leaſt Addreſs to her, yet her Vanity aſſured her, ſhe had made an abſolute Conqueſt of his Heart; and becauſe ſhe is an Heireſs, and has ſo many Courtiers already, ſhe ſaid, that ſhe was afraid he would fall a courting of her.

*La. Care.* 'Twas prodigiouſly ſilly, but very much of a Piece with the reſt of her Actions.        [*Bel. ſings.*

### AIR V.   The Collier has a Daughter.

'*Mongſt Men a Fop ſo ſtrange is,*
　*We hate them altogether;*
*A Coquette's only Change is,*
　*The one Sex for the other.*

#### II.

*The Men then can't but jeſt them;*
　*If otherways, they flatter,*
*For ſure they muſt deteſt them,*
　*And ſcorn their idle Clatter.*

*Enter a Servant.*

*Serv.* Madam, the Heireſs of *Kingiles* is come to wait upon you.

*La. Care.* Conduct her in. And now, *Belinda*, let us ſhift our Humour, my Dear, from a Serious to a Gay.

*Bel.* With all my Heart, for I can never be at a Loſs to change into my natural Humour.

*La. Care.* But here's the Heireſs.

*Enter*

*Enter the Heiress.*

*Heir.* Your Servant, Ladies, I hope I han't interrupted you in any fine Subject, before it was fully discuss'd.

*La. Care.* Not in the least, Madam; I hope you are well this Morning.

*Heir.* At your Ladyship's Service, and, as the Country People say, expecting to hear the same from you——Miss *Bele,* How do you do, my Dear?

*Bel.* Always to serve you, Madam; I thank God I have got Abundance of Health and good Humour, which I take to be the two chief Blessings of Life.

*Heir.* Ay——But Health, without some of the Diversions of Life, wou'd be but very insipid——Now, a Ball, an Assembly, or a Play, serves to make it agreeable; if it were not for these, our good Humour would degenerate into Melancholy, and our Health into a Weariedness of Life—— How should we spend the tedious Winter Nights, or how propose to put the Time off more agreeably, in an Afternoon, than at our Toilet? O, those dear, dear Assemblies, those Time-consuming Plays and Balls! I can never forgive any Body that does not place the chief Happiness of their Life in them.

*Bel.* But do you consider, Madam, that all these Diversions which you have mentioned, are not absolutely necessary for Happiness; for I am apt to believe, that the Generality of People in low Life, enjoy more Happiness than those in a higher Sphere.

*Heir.* Ay, ay, but I don't mean all that——I mean only, that, I assure you, they are always a very great Happiness to me: And won't you allow, Miss *Bele,* that a Play is a very innocent and instructing Diversion——I'm sure I have her now; for I've seen her very often at the Play. [*Aside.*

*Bel.* Nay, Madam, I never denied a good Play to be both innocent and instructing, where the Characters are well drawn. But the Taste of the Age is so prodigiously vitiated, that there is no Encouragement for any Thing that Folks of common Sense ought to think worth While to look at.

*Heir.* Why, really, Madam, the Taste is vitiated, as you say; but don't you think, my Dear, that *Harlequin* is a most entertaining Character.

B

*La. Care.* Ha, ha, ha.

*Bel.* Really, Madam, you have faved us the Trouble of giving you an Inſtance of the Folly of the Age, in pointing out one to us. Can there be any Thing more ridiculous, and foreign to the true Deſign of the Stage, which is to. repreſent the Virtues and Vices of Mankind, than, inſtead of them, to introduce a confus'd Rabble with antick Dreſſes, that only teach us to tranſform ourſelves into a Dog, an Ape, or a Lion : In ſhort, my Dear, the one ſeems to me, to be the meer Invention of the brute Creation, and the other, that of a reaſonable Soul.                                    [*ſings.*

### AIR VI.  A Jigg-Drouth.

*The Folks of Faſhion,*
*They ſcorn to trouble or vex their Brains,*
   *To view thoſe Paſſions*
*Writ in Ben. Johnſon or Shakeſpear's Strains.*
### II.
*Our Ladies pretty,*
*Who ſpend their Time in adoring their Glaſs,*
   *Swear Harliquin's witty,*
*And every fine Poet's a ſilly dull Aſs.*
### III.
*Fine Flights of Fancy,*
*They tell you are dull, and full of Chagrin,*
   *And the Harliquin Prancy,*
*Outwits them, and is the ſole Cure for their Spleen.*
### IV.
*For once peruſe them,*
*And let common Senſe judge a handſom writ Play,*
   *And you'll no more abuſe them,*
*But throw thoſe ſilly mean Tricks all away.*

*Heir.* Fy, fy, Miſs *Bele*, you han't the Taſte Alamode. I aſſure you, I have heard above Half a Dozen Perſons of Quality ſay the very ſame Thing ; and I never heard it contradicted.

*Enter Sir* Robert *introducing Mr.* Trimmer *to the Ladies. He ſalutes.*

*Sir Rob.* This is Lady *Careleſs*, Couſin.

*Trim.* Madam, your moſt obedient, humble Servant. [*Salutes her and the reſt*] Gad's my Life, Couſin, I think
you

you have your House planted with Angels; and an't I
a damnable lucky Fellow, who have not been in Town
thefe three Months, and, at my firft Entrance, to meet
with Three fuch pretty Creatures? I can tell you, it is a
good Omen — and to return the Ladies Favour, I fwear
to get drunk with Bumpers to their Healths ere Night.

*Heir.* You are full of Compliments, Sir.

*Trim.* Not in the leaft, Madam, for *Bacchus* himfelf
could not tofs your Health with that Grace it deferves
— Icod I think that was pretty well faid.      [*Afide.*

*La. Care.* Come Ladies, will you pleafe to walk into
the next Room, for our Tea waits us.   [*Ex. feverally.*

**SCENE III.** *Before* Sandy Buckram's *Door, enter Cook,
Butler, and Coachman, with Bottles in their Hands.*
                                          [Coach. *fings.*

**A I R VII.**   I met a pretty Wench.

*Once on a Summer's Morn, I went out to take the Air,
And I met a Wench upon a Bank, fo lovely and fo fair,
That I cou'd not mifs but ask her, why fhe wander'd there.*

**II.**

*She turn'd about, and threw up her pretty rolling Eyes,
With a Look fo gay; then did fhe fay, I'll not make you
          fo wife,
But I could not think of lofing, my pretty, pretty Prize.*

**III.**

*Then with a forward Mein, as I catch'd her in my Arms,
Upon near Approach, I found my Heart made Captive to
          her Charms,
And, to eafe my Flame, I ask'd her, what wou'd be the
          Terms.*

**IV.**

*But finding that fhe fcorn'd any mercenary Way,
O Sir, fays fhe, it is in vain, whatever you can fay,
For I am bound upon my Confcience, ftill to fay you, Nay.*

**V.**

*But when I further ask'd her, her Coynefs to ceafe,
As I kifs'd her clofe, and preft her hard, fhe yielded by De-
          grees,
And I then began to think, how my Paffion to releafe.*

                                              **VI. I**

### VI.

*I took her in my Arms, and I laid her on the Grass,*
*And we toy'd there a little while, her Coyness grew less.*
*Then we kiss'd until we wearied, the rest you'll easy guess.*

*Omnes.*  Tal lal, de lal, &c. *Sandy Buckram, Sandy,*
*Sandy,* hallo, Boy, hallo.

[*Knocks at the Door.*

*Enter* Sandy *opening the Door, and* Jean *pulls him back a-*
*gain, and comes out before him; he follows her.*

*Coach.* O, Mris. *Buckram,* we are glad to see you; and,
having all Three stole away for a little, we are come
with an honest Design, to drink merrily until these Bottles of Stout be at an End.

*Jean.* Thou art good a Boy, *Jack,* and thou art very
welcome; but, Gentlemen, I hope I need not make an
Excuse for pulling my Husband back again, when he was
coming out before me —— I assure you, it was out of no
Ambition to be out before him, but only Curiosity to see
who it was at the Door.

*Coach.* There was no Occasion for that Caution, Mris.
*Buckram;* we all know you well enough.

*Jean.* I assure you I han't the least Pride, for I hate
Pride above every Thing.

*Buck.* Nay, nay, Gentlemen, you must excuse me, for,
I must say, my Wife has no Pride at all, and she is always very obedient to me in every Respect, and ——

*Jean.* And, Sirrah, that's a Lie. Obedient, quoth-a, as
if we poor Women were always Slaves. Pray, Gentlemen, excuse me, I don't like to see a Man ill-manner'd,
or ill-natur'd; I hate ill Nature above every Thing, for
I always love to be in a merry Humour myself; but if you
please to come in —— I hope you will pardon me for
detaining you so long without Doors. [*Exeunt, and all re-*
*turn at another Door.* Sandy *introducing them, sings.*

**A I R VIII.** Buckram's *own Tune set by* Matthew
Briggs.

*Welcome, my Friends, to poor* Sandy Buckram's *House,*
*For tho' People call me, a silly* Prick the Louse,

*My*

*My Vote flands as good, on the Election Day,*
*As any of the Trade, and has as much to fay.*
*The firft that e'er comes, and gives Sandy a Boufe,*
*His Caufe, right or wrong, he will never lofe;*
*Our Deacon, in chufing the Provoft, does vote;*
*The Provoft, with Statefmen, may join in a Plot;*
*Then, Lads, have a Care, don't with Sandy debate,*
*Or elfe I will ftand up, and vote for the State.*
*When pothering Time comes, of a Bribe I'll be fure;*
*We'll excife you to Death, and give Penfions to W——*

Come, Gentlemen, pray let's be merry, for I affure you you are all very welcome, and our Wife will be here immediately with the Tankard.

*But.* Ay, but, *Sandy*, this is but an Introduction to our Mirth, Boy; for we have made Provifion for a fine Supper againft Night, and a large Bowl of Punch, and we defign to have it in your Houfe.

*Buck.* A fine Supper in our Houfe! Od's my Life, with all my Heart; and then I know my Wife will allow it, for I have often heard her fay, that fhe loved a fine Supper very much. A fine Supper, did not you fay?—Od I am very hungry—the very Name of it makes my Mouth water—for a fine Supper is a very fine Thing.

*Enter* Jean *with the Tankard and Bottles.*

*Coach.* O, but here comes our Beer; and, upon my Word, Mris. *Buckram*, you are in a very becoming Apparel to-Day.

*Jean.* Thank you, *Jack*, for your Compliment; but I hate all Manner of Affectation; yet I can't fay but I fuit any Kind of Drefs very well.

*Coach.* Before we begin to drink, Lads, I think it wou'd do beft to open our Affair to Mris. *Buckram*.

*Cook.* With all my Heart. We have made a Provifion for a fine Supper to-Night, Mris. *Buckram*, and becaufe we cou'd not ufe Freedom enough in our own Houfe, we were defigning to make merry with you.

*Jean.* O! Gentlemen, you know you're always welcome to me; but then you muft promife to difmifs again'ft Twelve o 'Clock, becaufe, if I fit up later, it fo incommodes me the next Day, that—not but, if you're inclin'd to take my *Sandy* with you, and make merry a

longer

longer Time —— I shan't be angry. That was well put in,
for then I shall have an Opportunity with Sir *Robert ;* but
mum for that. [*Aside.*

*Omn.* O! Mris. *Buckram,* we won't disturb you.

*Buck.* Now, Gentlemen, I appeal to you all, if I been't
a very happy Fellow. Did you ever see more Modesty and
Complaisance ? O! she's a sweet Creature.

*Jean* Well, *Sandy,* I never heard you speak more to
the Purpose in my Life ; and really, I must say, I hate e-
very Thing that's immodest, prodigiously —— But, Gentlemen, if you'll send your Provision, all Things shall be in
Readiness against Night.

*Coach.* It shall be done ; and now, Mr. *Butler,* pray
give us a Toast.

*But.* With all my Heart, and I hope Nobody will refuse it. Success to our merry Meeting, and the Health
of all the Company.

[*Before he drinks, the Coachman sings.*

### AIR IX. Prince of *Orange's* Rant.
*Let our Mirth abound,*
*And we'll toss the Cups around,*
*And we'll rant, and we'll roar, till we die, brave Boys.*
#### II.
*For every anxious Thought that is found*
*In our Breast, does proceed from our Fears, brave Boys ;*
*Then let our Voices each other resound,*
*With our Cups we will drive away Cares, brave Boys.*

[*While he drinks, the rest sing the Chorus, and dance a Reel.*
*Sandy Buckram endeavours to join the other two, but*
*Jean pulls him away, and takes his Place ; he dances alone.*
*Then the Cook takes the Tankard, and the Coachman sings.*]

### AIR X. Ditto.
*Our Polly is a Jade,*
*But a pretty little Maid,*
*Tho' I love, yet she laughs me to Scorn, brave Boys ;*
#### II.
*Yet now I swear, that I will no longer bear*
*With her Frowns, but I'll make myself free, brave Boys ;*
Come

*Come then let us drink, till we drown every Care*
*In a Bumper of Wine, as you see, brave Boys.*

[*The same as before. Then the Coachman takes the Tankard and sings.*]

## AIR XI. *Ditto.*

*The Lassie that's free,*
*She's a Damsel for me,*
*And I'll clasp the kind Wench in my Arms, brave Boys;*
### II.
*But for the Sluts that are surly and sour,*
*Let them all go be hang'd in a String, brave Boys,*
*For they're nought but a Pack of fantastical Whores;*
*And so here's a Health to the King, brave Boys.*

[*Chorus as before. Then Buckram takes the Tankard, and begins to sing; but his Wife frowns at him; he stays immediately, and gives it to her, and she sings.*]

## AIR XII. *Ditto.*

*Our Ladies in Town,*
*The black, fair, and brown,*
*Wou'd they dress but as simple as I, brave Boys.*
### II.
*Then, then, you would see what poor Figures they make*
*Without Paint, when they languish, they're pale, brave*
*    Boys;*
*Without Hoops let them toss, but their Tails will not shake,*
*But a Beauty like mine never fails, brave Boys.*

[*Chorus, &c. Buckram takes the Tankard, and sings.*]

## AIR XIII. *Ditto.*

*Since Life is but short,*
*Let us merrily sport*
*And rejoyce, since it lasts not long, brave Boys.*
### II.
*But have a Care in the Choice of your Wife,*
*For on that lies your Crisis of Fate, brave Boys;*
*You may chance to get One that will rusle your Life,*
*And engrave her Commands on your Pate, brave Boys.*
                                    SCENE

### SCENE IV. *Enter* Tom *following* Mally.

*Tom. Mal, Mal, Mal,* Where doft thou run, my Dear?

*Mal.* Ha!—on my Word you furprifed me, Mr. *Thomas.* But how I have the Honour of feeing you this Morning?

*Tom.* Faith, my Dear, you know it is an Honour you may always command; but how you came by it at prefent, is in Obedience to my Mafter's Commands. I came with his humble Refpects to Sir *Robert* and his Lady, to tell them he defigns to wait on 'em this Morning; and, you may be fure, the Expectations of feeing my dear *Mal*, haftened the Meffage very much. Come, prithee, *Mal*, let me have a Kifs for my Pains. [*Kiffes her.*

*Mal.* But pray, Mr. *Thomas*, Can't you guefs at the Reafon of thefe frequent Vifits of Mr. *Rover*'s, to our Houfe, for of late they have been much more than ordinary.

*Tom.* Mum—for that, Child, I dare not tell you—my Honour lies upon't.

*Mal.* Your Honour—really, Sir, I think I'm as much to be trufted with your Honour, as you are with mine.

*Tom.* How's that, my Dear—for you know I never had more than your Hand or your Lips.

*Mal.* Ay, but I'll give you more; I'll give you my Lips again, and my Hand in Promife of my Heart.

*Tom.* Will you? Nay, then my Mafter's Secrets [*kiffes her*] are in a fair Way to be difcovered; for that Kifs is enough to bribe a Lawyer from his Fee, or a Courtier to be honeft.

*Mal.* Nay, I hope it fhall not betray him, but rather do him a Service; and, if you will deal honeftly and fincerely with me, I have a Secret to balance yours, and perhaps I may intruft you with it, for I defign that we fhould both be ufeful to one another, in carrying on this Affair, that it may end to our Advantage.

*Tom.* Why, faith, *Mal*, you begin to talk very reafonably, and I really was defigned to trifle with you about it, but fince you are upon Honour, I'll be ingenuous, and, in plain Words, let you know, Mr. *Rover* has a Defign upon Lady *Carelefs*, to promote which, I have difcovered a Secret which no Body would fufpect.

*Mal.*

*Mal.* Pray, what can that be ?

*Tom.* T'other Day, as I went to call for some of my Master's Clothes, at *Sandy Buckram*'s, the Back Door that leads to his Workhouse being open, I went in, and hearing some Body whisper in the next Room, I had the Curiosity to peep ; and who shou'd be there, but Sir *Robert* toying with *Sandy*'s Wife ; he was very pressing, and she a little shy, but it was only to squeeze a little Money out of him ; at length I overheard him promise her Twenty Guineas, and immediately there was an Agreement made against this Night, betwixt Twelve and One, for she said, by that Time, she expected to pick a Quarrel with her Husband, and turn him out of Doors.

*Mal.* It was a very reasonable Expectation she had, I must own ; and, to give you all that I have to say, in few Words, my Lady *Careless* is a Woman of such strict Honour, that I am very certain, whatever Time he spends that Way, is but lost. Now, her Cousin *Belinda*, a Girl of the best Sense in *Edinburgh*, is desperately in Love with Mr. *Rover* ; however, you must not tell him this, for I am *Belinda*'s Confident in the Affair, and I would not, for the World, he should know of it ; but if we could manage Affairs so, that all Parties would be pleased, we should certainly find our Account in it.

*Tom.* Well said, *Mal*—Why, really I think the Design is good, and I don't in the least despair of Success, but, in order to that, it will be absolutely necessary to disappoint Sir *Robert*, which, with a little Invention, won't be very difficult ; but we'll consult about it more fully, and so, my dear *Mally*, give me your Hand. [*Sings.*

**A I R  XIV.** *At the Tree I shall suffer, &c.*
*I'll run through the World with* Polly,
*And protect her from all Melancholy.*
*Mal. Whate'er Dangers may come,*
*I'll still hold by my* Tom,
*Both. And we'll always be merry and jolly.* [*Exeunt.*

**S C E N E  V.** *Sir* Robert*'s Garden.*
Enter Rover *with* Lady Careless, *and* Trimmer *with the Heiress.*

*La. Care.* It was hard that Miss *Bele* was obliged to leave us so soon, for I am mightily in Love with that Girl's

C                                                    Com-

Company. She has so much good Humour, and smart
Wit, that wherever she is, let the Company be never so
flat, every Thing she says is full of Life and Spirit.

*Rov.* Yes, Madam, every Body acknowledges *Belinda*
to be a very accomplished young Lady.

*Heir.* I don't know, Sir, but I think there are a great
many other Ladies in Town, that have a much better Notion of Dress than Miss *Bele.* Don't you think so, Mr.
*Trimmer?*

*Trim.* Yes, Faith, Madam, it is my Opinion.

*Rov.* That may be, Madam; but I hope her Notion of
Dress does not in the least derogate from her good Sense.

*Heir.* I ask your Pardon, Sir, I thought you had meant
Dress.

*Rov.* Not at all, Madam.

*Heir.* [*Turning to* Trimmer, *while Rover talks aside to*
*Lady* Careless] Simple Fellow!——

*Trim.* Why, Faith, Madam, betwixt you and I—— he
is a simple Fellow——He might have had more Manners.

*Heir.* [*Angrily*] To my Face!——I can't endure to be
contradicted.

*Trim.* Pray, Madam, don't be discomposed; but if you
think yourself anyways affronted, I beg you would do me
the Honour to tell me——for those enchanting Looks have
so captivated my Heart, that he is a dead Man, if your
next Breath pronounce him so.

*Heir.* Ha! a lucky Hint that——he shall receive a Challenge immediately. [*Aside*] I cannot return the Favour you
have offered——but a Lady's Reputation, Sir, is not to be
dallied with; and if you will please to remove at a little
farther Distance from them, and take a Walk thro' the
Garden, we'll consult what is to be done.

*Trim.* With all my Heart, Madam——Pray Heaven she
don't take me at my Word. [*Aside*]

*Exeunt* Trimmer *and* Heiress; *then Lady* Careless *and Mr.*
Rover *come forward.*

*Rov.* Upon my Word, Madam, you push the Argument
so close, that, by and by, I am afraid I shall be at a
Loss to answer: But to give you another Reason, which
I think very solid, against Matrimony, there is a Promise
which every one must make at Marriage, that I don't believe any one knows, positively, whether it is in his Power

to keep or not, and that is, confining his Affections to one
Woman; for it is not impossible, but, one Time or other,
when those Charms which he once adored, are rendred familiar to him, another fair One might captivate his Heart,
and make him lothe what once he doted on.

*La. Care.* I own, Sir, there's a good deal of Reason in
that Objection; but altho' I should allow, that it very
often happens, yet I scarcely imagine you will say, that
it should be so.

*Rov.* If I were of Opinion that it should be so, I af-
sure you, Madam, I wou'd have no Objection to Matrimony; but I never yet could condescend to be guilty of
any Thing that I was conscious was ungenerous, and that
is undoubtedly such, to give one my Hand and Promise,
in what I can't be certain of performing.

*La. Care.* And for that same Reason, if there was any
Possibility of bringing you to it, I am apt to believe you'd
make a very kind Husband.

*Rov.* I can't interpret that any otherwise, Madam, than
a Banter, since Sir *Robert* had much more to boast of, in
any Respect, than I have.

*La. Care.* Whatever is done as to that, can't be undone again; and I think it is carrying ill Nature a great
deal too far, because I know one of the Sex is ungenerous,
to think they are all so. No, Sir, I assure you, that is
not the Case.

*Rov.* Nay, then, Madam, to speak sincerely, and return the Compliment, I don't know what I might have
done, had I been in Sir *Robert*'s Place. But what is become of the Heiress and Mr. *Trimmer.*

*La. Care.* Gone to take a Walk through the Garden, I
fancy.

*Rov.* Well, Madam, suppose we should take a View
of the Garden; and as we pass along by those Banks of
Flowers, to make Love in romantick Style, methinks,
would be very entertaining.

*La. Care.* To divert a little Time, with all my Heart,
Sir. Will you please to begin?

*Rov.* Yes, Madam.

*See,* Celia, *how* Narcissus *smiles;*
*It has no cunning Art or Wiles,*

But,

*But, as it spreads its beauteous Flower,*
*It sends its Odours through the Bower;*
*So let my Fair, while in her Prime,*
*Employ her Charms, not trust to Time,*
*Whose envious Power may blast that Face,*
*That now inchants with such a Grace;*
*For when those blooming Looks are o'er,*
*You will be importun'd no more.*
*Pray, Celia, scorn those trifling Arts,*
*By which mean Beauties conquer Hearts;*
*Tho' form'd by Nature's utmost Skill,*
*Don't exercise that Power to kill.*

La. Care. *Tho' Celia scorns each poor Design,*
*What Damon asks, she can't resign.*
*Narcissus gives the Fields their Due,*
*But this is what its bound to do.*
*Cease Damon, then, those amorous Strains,*
*Nor urge what Celia's Soul disdains.*

Rov. *Tell me, shou'd Celia heap up Charms,*
*All Nature's Stock, for Strephon's Arms,*
*Whilst, in Return, th' ungenerous Swain,*
*Treats the poor Nymph with cold Disdain.*

And, to be quickly over with our Romanticks, Marriage
is nothing but a Ceremony; and when once the Reason,
why it was made, is no more, I see no Reason why it ought
not to be forgotten. By Heavens — I can't look upon
you without being transported. O let me fly into your
Arms, my Life, my Soul! [*Sings.*

AIR XV. Ye Beaux of Pleasure.

Rov. *O, charming Creature,*
*How does each Feature*
*Exceed e'en Nature*
  *In Beauty and Charms?*

II.

La. Care. *How can that be, Sir,*
*When that you see, Sir,*
*He still flies me, Sir,*
  *To others Arms?*

III.

Rov. *Since he denies thee,*
*Pray, Celia, try me,*

*And*

*And do not fly me;*
*Ah fly no more.*
### IV.

*La. Care.* *But, Sir, remember*
    *He's still Pretender,*
    *I can't surrender;*
        *Therefore give o'er.*      [*Exit.*

*Rov.* I must follow her,
*And try by various Arts to win her Heart,*
*To play the wary cunning Lover's Part;*
*And yet, methinks, there's something in her Face,*
*That cries aloud — Virtue can't bear Disgrace.*    [*Exit.*

End of the First Act.

---

# ACT II. SCENE I.

*The Street before* Buckram's *House.* Buckram *appears*
*at the Window at Work.* Trimmer *following* Tom.

#### Trimmer.

HIST — hist! I ask your Pardon, Sir. Do you want any Money?

*Tom.* Pray, Sir, no Ceremonies, there needs no Excuse for that: But what must I do for it?

*Trim.* Why, what will you do for as much Money as will make you drunk for a Month every Night?

*Tom.* Any Thing in Honour, Sir.

*Trim.* Faith, Friend, I am glad to hear it. You say you are a Man of Honour; it was just such a one I was enquiring after, for you must know, that I have very unluckily engaged myself in a Point of Honour, that I han't all the Inclination in the World to go thro' with.

*Tom.* What may that be, Sir?

*Trim.* Being in Company with some Ladies, this Morning, one of them thought herself affronted, because she was contradicted by a young Fellow they call Mr. *Rover;* and, upon this, taking me for a Man of Honour and Courage, tips me the Wink to take a Walk thro' the Garden with
                                 her,

her, and there, in a long Harangue of pathetick Expreſ-
ſions, ſhe lays before me the Wrongs ſhe had ſuffered ; and
then, ſays ſhe, Sir, a Lady's Reputation is not to be dallied with.   This, you know, obliged me to offer her my
Service ; ſhe takes me at my Word, and inſiſts upon
ſending him a Challenge to meet me at the *Duke's Walk*
To-morrow Morning ; and pray, Sir, ſays ſhe, don't o-
mit to let him know whoſe Cauſe it is that you eſpouſe.

*Tom.* This is lucky to a Minuet. [*Aſide*]  Indeed, Sir,
I can't blame the Lady much, in pitching upon you.   I
aſſure you, Sir, you have all the Looks of a Man of Courage: You cock your Hat briskly, and wear a Sword ; and,
let me tell you, no Man ought to wear a Sword, but he
that can manage it.

*Trim.* Ay, ay, ſo I am a Man of Courage, and I like
Fighting well enough — but I'm indifferent about it, for
all that.

*Tom.* Yes, yes, Sir, as you ſay — A Man may like
Fighting well, but be indifferent about it, for all that.

*Trim.* Ay, — But to come to the main Buſineſs.   I
have the Challenge in my Pocket, ſeal'd up in a Letter,
with a Purſe and ſome Guineas, and, if you will take the
Affair in Hand, they are both at your Service.

[*Preſents them to him, he takes them.*

*Tom.* Sir, I'll do your Buſineſs for you.   I know the
Fellow very well ; he is a great Coward ; and I have known
him engaged in Half a Dozen ſuch Scrapes, and he was always obliged to beg Pardon, and allow himſelf to be
drubb'd.   You ſhall ſee how I will — uſe him.

*Trim.* A Coward, did you ſay ? — I hate a Coward, and
I'll drub the Fellow myſelf.   I have ſuch a Regard to a
Man of Honour, that I never would fight any one but a
Coward.   I love a Man of Honour — and I hate a Cow-
ard — a Coward !   But do you think that he'll yield up his
Sword at the firſt Bluſter, or ſo, for I ſhould not care to
put myſelf to the Trouble of, of —

*Tom.* Truſt me for that, Sir, and I'll engage he ſhall ;
and, as a Puniſhment upon me, if it fail, never truſt me a-
gain.   But what if you ſhould beg the Favour of the Lady,
to be at ſome convenient Diſtance, upon *Salisbury* Crags,
to bear Witneſs of our Victory.

*Trim.*

*Trim.* With all my Heart; and I know she is so fond of the Thing, she'll never refuse it: But pray who shall we have for a third Man, if there should be Occasion? for, to be sure, he'll bring one along with him, that perhaps may not be altogether so peaceable, so we had best have one concealed at some little Distance, to make every Thing sure; for I would not care for it at all, except every Thing were as sure as if it were done already.

*Tom.* There will be no great Danger in that: But, to make every Thing sure, as you say, it would not be amiss to have a little Help at Hand; and there is a Fellow lives in this House, of undaunted Courage, his Name is *Buckram.* O! I see him looking out at the Window, if you please I'll call him.

*Trim.* Ay, do, do.    [Tom *goes forward to the Window*]
*Tom.* Hup—hist, *Sandy Buckram!*
*Buck.* [*From the Window*] I'm your humble Servant, Mr. *Thomas*, and I'm glad to see you.    I have been busy at your Master's Clothes all this Morning, and they're almost finished.

*Tom.* Prithee be quiet with your Nonsense about Clothes, and come down here quickly; I have got a Purse of Gold, here, about a Challenge, and you are to be one—Haste, haste, come along.

*Buck.* A Purse of Gold about a Challenge, and I'm to be one—Whether is't to eat or drink?—But I'll be at him immediately.

*Tom.* [*To* Trim. *while* Buckram *is coming down*] You see, Sir, with what Cheerfulness he leapt down, whenever I spoke of a Challenge.

*Trim.* Yes, Faith, the Fellow has Courage in his Looks.
### Enter Buckram.
*Buck.* Od's my Life, Mr. *Thomas*, when are we to begin?
*Tom.* [*To* Trim.] Do you hear that, Sir? [Tom *to* Buckram, *aside.*] Now, *Buckram*, my Boy, you must pull up a good Heart.

*Buck.* Nay, I warrant you, I'll not fail—I'll eat for the Honour of the Taylors of the Head of the *Canongate* —But tell me, shan't we have both Meat and Drink?

*Tom.* Nay, but hear me out—Here's a Purse of Gold, that will afford us Meat and Drink in Abundance—But the Challenge is to fight, my Boy.

*Buck.*

*Buck.* Fight, my Boy!——O Lord, Mr. *Thomas*, I see a Gentleman going up to my House, to get the Measure of a Suit of new Clothes——and I can't stay, for my Wife——

*Tom.* Hold, hold, I tell you, [*pulling out the Purse*] Here's two Guineas for you, and that is more than you can make by a Suit of Clothes, and, when the Affair is ended, you shall have two more. [*He takes it*]

*Buck.* But, Mr. *Thomas*, do you expect to make me fight for this Money?

*Tom.* I never designed you should, only you must make this Fellow believe that you will, and that you are a Man of Honour and Courage: You must bluster, and talk big, nay, you must go to the Field too, but take my Word upon't you shan't fight.

*Buck.* Well, honest Mr. *Thomas*, I will take your Word upon't, and if your Business is only to bully, I'll fit you for that; nay, for that Matter, I love to fight as well as any Man, but I can't endure Blows.

*Tom.* [*To* Trimmer.] Sir, we ask your Pardon for detaining you so long, but it was necessary that I should inform my Friend, Mr. *Buckram*, in the Circumstances of the Affair.

*Trim.* I know it was. Well, Sir, I hope you are satisfied about it.

*Buck.* Satisfied, Sir —— I'm never better satisfied than when I'm hotly engaged in a Duel —— for Fighting is my daily Trade. That's no Lie, for I have a daily Skirmish with my Wife. [*Aside*] —— Where is my Sword and Buckler, Coat of Mail, and Cap of Steel!

*Tom.* Hold, hold, Mr. *Buckram*, 'tis not till To-morrow's Morning.

*Buck.* To-morrow! 'Tis a whole Age —— I'm on the Rack until the Time —— That's no Lie neither. [*Aside.*

[*Sings.*] **A I R XVI.** The Birth-Day.

*Come on, my merry Lads, with courageous Hearts,*
*And fight it out bravely, despising those Flirts,*
*That will boast of their Sense, and call one a Fool,*
*But let me see if they dare fight a Duel;*
*For where there is one to be found,*
*That will stand it out bravely, nor fly a Bit of Ground,*

*There*

*There is Twenty you'll see, more Cowards that be,*
*And value their Honour, no more than I do this Flea.*
                                        [Exeunt.

### SCENE II. Belinda's *Apartment.*

*Enter* Belinda *and* Rover.

*Bel.* Come along, Sir. You see I use my utmost Endeavours to divert you; and when ever our Discourse turns flat, if I can't change the Subject, I think the next best is, to change the Room; for Variety, you know, Sir, is the general Outcry of your Sex.

*Rov.* You might have said, of all rational Creatures, Madam; for Nature itself delights in Variety; but, let me tell you, that any one who proposes to spend his Life as I do, I mean, at Liberty, ought to beware of engaging too much with Beauty, Wit, and Humour, all at once, for that sometimes is found to be too prevalent for the most resolv'd of our Sex; and, upon my Word, Madam, there is not one amongst the few Acquaintances that I have, whom I dread Half so much as I do *Belinda.*

*Bel.* Still a little upon the Banter, Sir.

*Enter a Servant.*

*Serv.* Sir, your Servant desires to speak with you.

*Bell.* Bid him come in. [*Exit Servant.*] Perhaps, Sir, it is some Piece of Business, and you would incline for another Room.

*Rov.* Not that I know of, Madam. But here he comes.

*Enter* Tom.

*Tom.* [*Looking about him.*] None to overhear, I hope.

*Rov.* None but whom you see.

*Tom.* Well then, here is a Letter, which I don't doubt will divert you both; and you must know, that I am brib'd with Half a Dozen of Guineas, to perform the Contents, but I have persuaded him (with a great deal of Difficulty I must own) to do it himself; but then he insisted upon having a Thirds-Man, which I have taken Care is as great a Coward as himself. This is all that I have to tell you just now, the Letter will inform you of the rest. I hope, Sir, you will allow me to be gone, for I have a little Business upon my Hands.

D                                              *Rov.*

*Rov.* Well then, go your Ways. [*Exit* Tom] Now, Madam, for the Letter.                    [*Reads.*

SIR,

*YOU may remember, I had the Honour of seeing you this Morning at Sir* Robert Careless's *House, in Company with his and other two Ladies —— The prettiest of the Two, but whom I take to have the least Sense, by Name* Belinda, *went away; after she was gone, out of Design, I suppose, to please Lady* Careless, *and affront the other, you was not only lavish in your Commendations of her, before the other's Face, but had the Impudence to contradict her —— For which, Sir, I desire you would attend me, To-morrow's Morning, precisely at Four of the Clock, at the* Duke's Walk, *with a small Sword, and no other Weapon. From*

ANDREW TRIMMER.

N. B. *If you bring more than one along with you, I shall use you like a Scoundrel, for, upon Honour, I am to bring no more.*

P. S. *Pray take Notice, that this is at the particular Desire of the young Lady.*

*Rov.* Silly Scoundrel! Any one may know by his Postscript, that he's a Coward, to expose his Mistress thus; that very Thing plainly demonstrates, that he had no Inclination to it himself.

*Bel.* Why, really, his *N. B.* confirms it; for he has engag'd his Honour to bring but one, and is really to have Two.

*Rov.* Faith, Madam, it is doing him too much Honour, to spend any Time in talking about him; but from this you may plainly see, how often your Sex are mistaken in their Notions of ours. Any one that wears a Sword, and has a smart Look, passes for a Man of Courage; and a young Fellow who has as much Prudence in Conversation, as not to betray his Ignorance, is taken for one of solid Sense.

*Bel.* That, indeed, Sir, is the common Way of judging; and, generally speaking, they make the Appearance of the pretty Fellows of the Age, and yet are altogether
lazy,

lazy, indolent, and sluggish. Their whole Life is sacrificed to Diversions, and they think of nothing but —— O Lord, shall we go to the Play, the Assembly, or Ball, Tonight? They amuse themselves with Trifles in their Youth, and become a Prey to Ignorance in their old Age. [*Sings.*

AIR XVII. Whilst the Town's brimful of Folly.
*Troops of Beaux, in shining Dresses,*
*Croud to all those publick Places,*
   *Where the Ladies oft resort ;*
        II.
*All with painted ugly Faces,*
*Aping Smiles, make strange Grimaces,*
   *Try to catch each fair One's Heart,*
*All with painted ugly Faces, &c.*
   *But are Subject of their Sport.*

*Rov.* I'm afraid, Madam, I have intruded upon your good Humour too much, in making this Visit so long ; but I hope you will excuse me.
*Bel.* Upon Condition that the next shall be To-morrow, I will ; for you know, Mr. *Rover*, that I always deal very plainly , and, to tell you Truth, I am engaged this Night to Supper, else I would not have allowed you to go away so soon.
*Rov.* I return you Thanks, Madam, and I'll be sure to do myself the Honour to wait upon you To-morrow ; till then, your humble Servant. [*Exit.*
*Bel.* Sir, your Servant.
        *Sola.*
Well, if our Plots succeed, I shall be a happy Creature —— He has gain'd so much upon my Affections, that I shall never so much as think of another ; and if this Night proves favourable to our Designs, all shall end in happy Success. [*Sings.*

AIR XVIII. My Nanny-O.
*How does a blushing Virgin's Heart*
   *Exult with Hope, and shake with Fear?*
*She trys her Charms, and every Art,*
   *To bring the wish'd for Moment near.*
            But

But if some wild unlucky Turn,
     Should spoil our Plots and main Design,
The Heart before that leapt wou'd mourn,
     And in Despair away repine.          [*Exit.*

### SCENE III.   *Mally* and *Tom.*

*Tom.* Prithee, *Mally*, don't be in such a Haste, my Dear, for I han't got half Information about that Affair, and I shan't know how to behave in't.   Come, you shall give me a regular Rehearsal of it.

*Mal.* Well, then, do you remember what was the Substance of the two Letters, which we wrote, at Mr. *Rover*'s Desire, to the Heiress and Mr. *Trimmer*.

*Tom.* Yes, very well.

*Mal.* They are both delivered to the respective Persons, and they have swallowed the Bait like Two hungry Fishes; and I understand from the Heiress's Gentlewoman, there is nothing she is so fond of as a travell'd Beau.   All that you have to do, is to dress as such, and attend her To-morrow Morning early, by Six o' Clock.   Insist upon the Condition in the Letter, which is, to marry at first Sight.   Tell her, it is the Taste Alamode; prattle a little *French* to her, which I know you can do; wheedle her over, and she's yours in an Instant; and let me alone to play my Part with Mr. *Trimmer*.

*Tom.* Play your Part — Nay, *Mal*, I don't doubt but that you are capable to play your Part, with one Man, at any Time.   But what's next to be done, for I hope you don't design to marry them in Sincerity.

*Mal.* Hang Sincerity! let People be serious, who have nothing else to do.   No, no, Mr. *Rover* told us we must not do that.   But you know the Room that I have taken to entertain Mr. *Trimmer* in, is not far from the Heiress's Lodgings, and I have a Fellow disguis'd like a Parson, to wait and perform the Ceremony; and, as I am to go under the Name of your Sister, when ever you've gain'd your Point, you can easily persuade her to go along with you to your Sister's House, where, you can tell her, there will be all Preparation, and another Couple in the same Condition.

*Tom.* Well, well — Now I have it exactly, and, I warrant you, I'll manage well enough; but I must be gone to a merry Meeting in *Sandy Buckram*'s, and endeavour to play

the

the Cards so as to disappoint Sir *Robert*, for 'tis mainly upon that Account, that I accepted the Invitation from *Sandy* — Do you take Care, and mind your Cue about the other Affair.

*Mal.* Never doubt me — But remember that I am to meet Mr. *Rover*, at the Gate, exactly betwixt Twelve and One, and when ever he comes, I'll direct him to that Corner of the House where you are to watch — And pray let his Disappointment be as unmerciful as possible; it will the sooner reconcile him to Thoughts of Matrimony, which is the Design of the whole Scheme; and, as for my Part, since you talk'd of playing your Cards, I'll warrant you I shan't lose my Ten.

*Tom.* That's my pretty *Mal* — Come kiss me, and then let's about our Business. [*Kisses her.*

### AIR XIX. *Robin* shore in Har'st.

Mal. *Thus two Birds, when join'd,*
*Fly about the Forest,*
*Seeking where to find*
*Fog to build their Nest.*
#### II.
*Seek all around it,*
*Until they've found it,*
*And, when they've bound it,*
*Down they sit to rest.*
#### III.
Tom. *Thus, my pretty Mal,*
*If this ben't miscarried,*
*End our Troubles shall,*
*And we will be married.*
#### IV
Both. *Youth is fast running,*
*Old Age is coming,*
*Let's then be cunning,*
*To dispatch it fast.* [*Exeunt.*

**SCENE IV.** *Buckram's House. A covered Table with Supper upon it, and a large Bowl of Punch upon another.*

*Enter* Jean Buckram, *singing.*

**AIR**

AIR XX. King of *Damascus.*

*How will my Heart then leap with Joy,*
  *When I view the horn'd Creature,*
*Minding nothing but vain Joys;*
        *All his Life but Pain.*

**II.**

*Whilst I enjoy Store of Treasure,*
  *Neither whining nor repining,*
*But my Life all full of Pleasure,*
        *And must still remain.*

**III.**

*Since Knights are ravish'd with my Favour,*
*Each contending who shall have her,*
*I'll be modest in Behaviour,*
        *Store of Wealth to gain.*
        [Looking at herself in a Glass.

Methinks I look charmingly to Day—but so I always do, else why would a Knight, such a fine Gentleman—and so good a Judge of every Thing—fall in Love with me—But I must own he has a good Taste—Well, I don't believe any Woman upon Earth could have done more. I stood out against two Attacks, but it was impossible to withstand the Third, especially as I had the Temptation of so much Money—Ay, and that was irresistible—My Charms, I really think, are prodigiously inticing—but yet I may thank my own Cunning for Part of the Money—for I wrought him up nicely. O! how I tickled him—But mum for that; here comes our Company.

*Enter* Buckram *introducing* Cook, Butler, *and* Coachman.
                                    [Buck. *sings.*

AIR XXI. Let's be jovial.
*Ducks and Hens, and sumptuous Living,*
  *Punch, with all its Joys, are here;*
*Feel my Heart—feel how 'tis heaving*
*With Desire to taste our Chear.*

*Buck.* Come, my Lads, let's fall too—hang Ceremony.
*Omnes.* Ay, ay, hang Ceremony. [*They fall on.* Buckram *devours greedily.*                        *Coach.*

*Coach.* But, *Buckram*, they tell me that you can eat and sing both at once. Come, prithee let's have a Song.

*Buck.* Faith they do me Justice there, for I never sing better than when I am eating, because I eat very slow —— and I will give you a——[*Looking at his Wife*] but my Wife can sing a great deal better than I can do.

*Jean.* But since the Company desires it, you may sing a Song, *Sandy.*

*Buck.* May I, Troth with all my Heart.　　　[*sings.*

AIR XXII. Auld Sir *Simon* the King.
*In* Berwick *there liv'd a young Maid,*
　*Whose Beauty outshone the Day,*
*She was by a Youngster betray'd,*
　*Who led the poor Girl astray.*
**II.**
*And when some Years had past,*
　*And Beauty had yielded its Charms,*
*She past for a Maiden at last,*
　*In a silly old Batchelor's Arms.*
　　　　　　　　[A Knock at the Door.

*Jean.* Stop a little, *Sandy,* till I answer the Door. [*Exit.*

*Buck.* Oho, I can tell you who it will be; it is Mr. *Thomas,* for I invited him, and he promised to come, and I wish it may, with all my Heart, for he's a merry Fellow, I can tell you.

**Enter** Jean *and* Tom.

*Jean.* You see, Mr. *Thomas,* we are all very merry.

*Omnes.* Honest Mr. *Thomas,* welcome.

*Tom.* That's my merry Lads, I'm glad to see you, upon my Word.

*Buck.* [*Rising*] Will you please to take my Seat, [*sitting down*] but this is at the Foot of the Table. Pray, Gentlemen, make Room above there. [Jean *brings him a Seat, he sits down.*

*Jean.* Come, come, fall to; you see we are all busy, Sir.

*Tom.* Thank you, Mris. *Buckram,* and so I will. [*falls to.*

*Jean.* And, *Sandy,* do you go on with your Song.

*Buck.* Troth and so I will, *Jeany,* but I believe I had best begin it again.

　　　　　　　　　　　　　AIR

AIR XXIII. *Ditto.*

*In* Berwick *there liv'd, a young Maid,* &c.

### III.

*When first the poor Puppy began*
  *To court her, he ly'd like a Page,*
*He danc'd and he frisk'd, and he sung,*
  *And deny'd twenty Years of his Age.*

### IV.

*And when he had gained her Will,*
  *She clapt the Horns upon his Head;*
*Lord pity the silly old Fool,*
  *But there's Hundreds alive, tho' he's dead.*

[After the Song, they all rise and sing the Chorus.

*Buck.* And now, Gentlemen, I think we are very well sup'd. I hope we shall come at our Punch next——Shall I fill up——[*Jean frowns*] Gentlemen, Shall my Wife fill up the Glasses?

*Jean.* Gentlemen, I presume I may.

*Omnes.* O, yes, to be sure.  [*She fills the Glasses.*

*Tom.* Now, Gentlemen, let us have all the Company's Healths for the first Toast.

*Omnes.* All the Company's Healths.  [*Drinks.*

*Buck.* Od, it has a savoury Taste. But whose Health shall we drink next——for I love to drink Healths.

[Jean *fills.*

*Cook.* Faith, I'll tell you, we'll drink Liberty and Property, and no Excise.  [*They take up the Glasses.*

*Butler.* Nay, Gentlemen, pray excuse me there——for my Master is a Courtier, and I will not do that.

*Tom.* Pooh! Never quarrel about that. Do you consider that you are no Body's Servant just now——? besides, a Statesman himself can be honest over a Bottle. Come, let's have the Health.

*Omnes.* Liberty, &c.  [*All drink.* ]ean *fills again.*

*Buck.* Now, Gentlemen, suppose we should take our Breath a little; and if my Wife and the Company pleases, she and I shall entertain the Company with a new Catch.

*Omnes.* Ay, ay, pray do, Mris. *Buckram.*

*Jean.* Well, Gentlemen, since you desire it so earnestly, I'll do it, and so, *Sandy,* your Part is first, begin then.

*Buckram*

**AIR XXIV.** Beſſy Bell and Mary Gray.

Buck. *Dear* Nelly *thou art the* Queen *of our* Plain,
*And the* Nymphs *about envy thee;*
*I ſcorn their* Power, *to none I complain*
*But to thee, and pray do not deny me.*

## II.

*I'm* Robin, *well known to the* Country *round,*
*And my* Favour *is always intreated;*
*My* Deſigns *with* Succeſs *have always been crown'd,*
*Not one of them ever defeated.*

## III.

Jean. *Then, prithee now,* Robin, *of vaunting no more,*
*And begone to thoſe* Nymphs *you have gained;*
*Let every poor* Slut, *who inclines, be your* Whore,
*But, for my* Part, *I ſwear I diſdain it.*

## IV.

Buck. *Then farewel, Miſs* Saucy, *nor caſt ſuch an* Air,
*For a* Whore *tho' I meant not to make you,*
*There are Twenty of thoſe as handſom and fair,*
*So farewel for I henceforth forſake ye.*

## AIR XXV. Bartholomew Fair.

Jean. *Ah!* Robin, *why ſo quickly do you haſte away?*
*I meant not what I ſaid, ſo pray now ſtay;*
*If* Robin *forſake me, where, then, will poor* Nelly *fly,*
*I'll — go — no — where — elſe, but here I'll die.*

## AIR XXVI. Hay Makers.

Buck. *Smile, then, my pretty* Nell, *for this was but to try*
*thee;*
*Age ſhall not ſee the* Time, *when* Robin *will deny thee.*
Jean. *Ah did you know but how ſincerely I adore you,*
*How many were deſpis'd that ſigh'd and kneel'd be-*
*fore me.*

## II.

Buck. Nelly's *Eyes, with Surpriſe,*
*Made the* Swains *poor* Hearts *to riſe;*
*While they ſigh'd away ſhe flies;*
*In vain they did implore you.*

[All dance to the Tune.

Coach. *Faith, that was well done; but let's have t'other*
Health. [*All take their Glaſſes.*

E　　　　　　　　Tom,

*Tom.* Confusion to all Knaves, and every one his own Miftris's Health.

*Omnes.* Confusion, &c. [*Drink.*

*Jean.* *Sandy*, do you take the Charge of the Bowl, for I am quite wearied.

*Buck.* [*Running to the Bowl*] Pray, Gentlemen, don't you think my Wife is a fweet Creature? [*Fills the Glaffes, and fits down by the Bowl; he puts it to his Head.*

*Tom.* Now, Gentlemen, fince the Healths are fairly begun, I think it would be very proper to chufe a Prefes in the Company.

*Omnes.* Ay, ay, a Prefes in the Company.

*Buck.* [*Taking the Bowl from his Head*] Ay, ay, a Prefes in the Company. [*Drinks.*

*Coach.* And I don't think there can be a properer Perfon for the Purpofe, than the Landlord of the Houfe, for he's a Man of Learning, I can tell you.

[*Buckram taking the Bowl from his Head.*

*Buck.* Yes, Faith, with all my Heart, for I am a Man of Learning, as you — [*his Wife frowns*] but pray, Gentlemen, would not my Wife do a great deal better, for fhe's a Man of Learning too, I can tell you. [*Drinks again.*

*Butler.* You mean, a Woman of Learning, you Fool; but a Woman can't be Prefes in a Company.

[*Buckram taking the Bowl from his Head, and tipfy.*

*Buck.* A Woman, did you fay — ay, to be fure. I am a Man, that's one Thing, and Mr. *Thomas*, I hope you will ftand by me To-night, and I'll ftand by you To-morrow — Do you only obferve my Wife there, how dreadful fhe looks, when there is any Piece of Honour to be put upon me. am bloodily afraid of her, but if you will keep her off, you fhall fee what a brave Fellow I fhall be. [*Runs behind him and drinks.*

*Tom.* O, never mind that, Man; Mris. *Buckram*, is a very peaceable Woman. [*Standing between Sandy and her.*

*Jean.* I affure you, Gentlemen, 'tis contrary to my Inclination to difturb your Company; but — don't raife my Corruptions — you Dog.

[*Sandy ftarts, and fets down the Bowl.*

*Buck.* You fee fhe will talk; but pray, Gentlemen, know me as his Majefty, your — Prefes, and, in Deference to my Greatnefs, take up your Glaffes, and let my Health go round.

*Omnes.*

*Omnes.* The Prefes's Health in a Bumper. Huzza! [*All drink.*

*Buck.* Now, Mr. *Coachman*, by the Authority of a Prefes, I order you to fing that Song which you have, to the Tune of the new Minuet — for I love finging and drinking with all my Heart. [*Drinks.*

*Coach.* You fhall have that in a Moment. [*Sings.*

### AIR XXVII. Mifs MacLeod's Minuet.

*Wine, Wine, Wine, that chears the Soul,*
*Drowns every Thought — but fill up the Bowl.*
*While drinking, no thinking, while drinking, &c.*
*While drinking we're freed from all Controul.*

#### II.

*Free from tormenting Cupid's Pains,*
*Scorning to wear Celia's Chains.*
*If fhe's coy, coy, ftill coy, coy,*
*Yet coy, coy, ftill coy, coy,*
*I return her Frowns with Difdain.*
*If fhe will not, why, I care not; If fhe will not, &c.*
*If fhe will not, I'll find another, and her refrain.*

[In the Time of this Song, *Buckram* drinks once or twice, and gets drunk]

*Coach.* Gentlemen, this is one of the newest Songs in Town. I got it as a great Compliment from one of your great Beaux *Valets de Chambre.*

*Buck.* I agree with you altogether, Sir; and now, as I value Nobody, but ftill you muft ftand by me, Mr. *Thomas* — I fay, as I value Nobody, I'll give you my own Song, which is juft my Condition.

*Coach.* Ay, ay, let's have it. [*Buckram fings.*

### AIR XXVIII. Emperor's March.

*Come, merry Fellows, toft the Cups about;*
*Let dull Philofophers Myfteries find out,*
*Let them all confufe their Souls*
*About they know not what,*
*Whilft we the Day fhall drink away — in Pleafure.*

#### II.

*Thus we are furnifh'd againft all ftocking Cares,*
*And thus we will drown all trembling Thoughts of Fear:*
*And*

*And he that lives a wretched Life,*
*By Reason of a scolding Wife,*
*Let him take Heart, and beat her Buff* — *severely.*

### III.

*As for my own Part, I have a Wife at Home,*
*Whose practis'd in the Devil's Arts, and fears not what's*
        *to come ;*
*I'll vow and swear no Man can bear*
*Her nasty scolding Tongue,*
*Yet she presumes to beat my Buff* — *severely.*

### IV.

*But, brave Boys, I'll be no more a Slave,*
*And I'll slit up my Courage, you'll see how I behave ;*
*O, I'll tame her so, and lay her Pride,*
*Then tell her that I can't abide*
*The Stuff she prattles by my Side,* — *so boldly.*

*Jean.* [*Pulls out her Whip, and runs at* Buckram] I can
bear it no longer. Get out of my House, you Rascal.

        [Tom *holds her,* Buckram *runs to the Door.*
*Buck.* Treason, Treason, against his Majesty himself !
Pray, Gentlemen, guard your Preses.                    [Jean *sings.*

### A I R XXIX.    Drummore's Rant.

*Begone in Haste, you nasty Slave,*
*Or else your Head you shall not save*
*From Two good Fists, which here I have,*
        *Shall make you very sad upon't.*
*Buck.*    *In any Place I may grow rich,*
        *For with the Needle I can stitch ;*
*So fare you well, you nasty* —
        *I hope you will run mad upon't.*

                    [All run out except *Jean.*

*Jean.* Now, I think the Coast is clear, and 'tis just a-
bout the Time that Sir *Robert* promis'd to come. I know
he's a Man of Honour, and will stand to his Word — O,
how happy shall I be if he continues to love me, for I
shall always have Money in Abundance, and live plenti-
fully, and that foolish Puppy, my Husband, shall never
know how I come by it.                              [*Sings.*
                                              A I R

### A I R XXX. Dribles of Brandy.

*When I'm carousing all the Day,*
 *What care I what comes of Sandy ?*
*E'en let him do whatsoever he may,*
 *I'm for a Posset of Brandy.*

#### II.

*If I turn tipsy, and scold him well,*
 *May be he'll call me a Randy ;*
*But, if he likes, he may hang himself,*
 *I'm for a Posset of Brandy.*

#### III.

*When he gets drunk upon any Time,*
 *And my Command not attends to,*
*'Tis among Soundrels not worth the While,*
 *And this is all he pretends to.*

#### IV.

*Does it become such a silly Knave,*
 *Either to kiss or command me,*
*Since that I can make a Knight my Slave,*
 *So that he cannot withstand me.*

[A Knock at the Door.

Heark, Somebody knocks ; it can be Nobody else but Sir *Robert.* [Exit, *and* Tom *and* Buckram *appear at the Window.*

*Tom.* Now, *Sandy,* let us observe them, for I saw Sir *Robert* go to the Door this Instant.

*Buck.* —— Lord have Mercy upon us, and will he horn me, dost think ? But really, Mr. *Thomas,* I know you are an honest Gentleman, and you can't in your Conscience answer to see me cuckolded to my Face.

*Tom.* Never mind that ; there shall be no Fear of that, but you must be sure to do exactly whatever I desire you.

*Buck.* Yes, yes, I'll warrant you for that.

*Tom.* But hush, here they come.

##### Enter Sir Robert *and* Jean.

*Jean.* I hope, Sir *Robert,* you will excuse me, for introducing you into this nasty confus'd Room, but the Bed in the other is not just in such Readiness as I would have it, and while you undress, I'll step aside a little, and make it ready. But remember ——

*Sir.* O, the Money you mean ; here it is, Child.

*Buck.* Yes, yes —— and in a little Time my Horns will be planted a Yard deep.                                          *Jean.*

*Jean.* You are a very generous Gentleman, Sir *Robert*, always going about doing Acts of Charity ; but if you please to get ready, I'll be again in an Instant. [*Laying down the Money in their View*] I fancy it will be safe enough there, — until I get a little more Time. [*Aside.*

[*Sir* Robert *begins to strip,* Jean *goes out.*

*Tom.* Sandy, Sandy, get down and knock at the Door, and I'll wait here, and see how they behave.

*Buck.* Ay, ay, but you must stand by me, tho'.

[*Goes down.*

*Tom.* Never doubt that —— Now would some lucky Hit of Fortune favour my Design —— but we'll see what this produces. [*A Knock at the Door.*

*Enter* Jean *hastily.*

*Jean.* Alas, Sir *Robert*, what shall we do ? there is Somebody at the Door.

*Sir.* Have you no Place that I might be conceal'd in ?

[*Knocks again.*

*Jean.* Troth, that's well thought on, there is a large Chest in the Closet, which will hold you ; haste, come into it, and I'll lock it upon you.

*Sir.* With all my Heart. [*Exeunt. Still knocking.*

*Tom.* Sandy, hearkye, Man. I've got a Project in my Head, which will nettle them bravely ; I'll about it immediately. [*Goes down.*

*Enter* Jean *running across the Stage.*

*Jean.* Coming, coming. [*Exit, and returns with* Buckram] So you say you must carry home Mr. *Rover*'s Clothes. Well, give me the Key where they ly, and I'll fetch them to you —— I must not say any more just now, for Sir *Robert* is hearing me. [*Aside.*

*Buck.* Here it is. [*Exit* Jean] I have given her a wrong Key, according to Mr. *Thomas*'s Direction.

*Enter* Tom *with two Porters, to the Closet.*

*Tom.* Take this in all Dispatch, and carry it to Sir *Robert Careless*'s Lodgings ; deliver it to the Servants, and tell it is foreign Goods for their Master, and I'll follow you immediately, and see you paid. [*They take it up, and Exeunt*] Now, *Sandy*, do you undeceive her, give her the right Key, and get the Clothes, and follow me. [*Exit* Tom.

*Buck.* [*To* Jean *within*] Have you got the Clothes yet ?

*Jean.*

*Jean.* I can't find them, I fancy they muſt be in the other Cheſt.

*Buck.* Well —— here is the Key of it, pray be quick, [*Goes in a little, and gives her the Key*] if I durſt but take up the Money —— but I'll leave that until I am ready to run away.

*Jean.* Here they are, *Sandy.*

*Buck.* Have you lock'd the Cheſt?

*Jean.* Not yet.

*Buck.* Well, do it then, and give me the Key. [*Exit* Jean. Buckram *throws off his Coat and Veſt, and puts on the fine Clothes; then takes up the Money*] Let *Rover* go to the Devil, if he has a Mind——for I'm a Gentleman, and I'll drink and ſwear with the beſt of them. [*Exit* Buckram.

*Enter* Jean.

*Jean.* Here is your Key——What, gone already——Ha, my Money gone too——Villain, Raſcal, if I had him, I'd pull out his Eyes. [*Goes towards the Cloſet, and miſſes the Cheſt*] Loſt ——undone, ruin'd, Heavens——Death, Murder ——Robbery and Oppreſſion. I'll ſearch over all the Town for him; I'll make him pay for it. [*Exit in a Fury.*

SCENE V. *Sir* Robert Careleſs's *Houſe.*

*Enter Lady* Careleſs, Belinda, *and* Mal.

*La. Care.* Dear *Belinda,* I'm in ſuch a Condition, betwixt Hope and Fear, that, if I was not ſupported by your good Company, I believe I ſhould fall into Vapours: But tell me, *Belinda,* don't you think that Men are ſad deceiving Creatures?

*Bel.* Generally ſpeaking, Madam, I do; and I know that there are a great many who make it a common Practice to make Love to every young Girl that will hear them, and have a certain Pride in ſwearing, to Half a Dozen different Ones, what they deſign to perform to none of them.

*La. Care.* True, indeed, Madam, we ought always to be very much upon our Guard, yet I ſincerely believe, that no Body has more Generoſity than Mr. *Rover,* and if once he was brought to be reconcil'd with Matrimony, he would make you exceedingly happy; but, as for my own Part, my Hopes are exceedingly ſmall. [*Sings.*

AIR

AIR XXXI.   Cuſtom prevailing.

*In chuſing a Husband, I ſure have been blind,*
*And in trying Methods to prove him,*
*For were he not cruel, unconſtant, unkind,*
*There's no Mortal, ſure, but would love him.*

II.

*But when he looks on me with ſuch a Diſdain,*
*My Heart it ſwells high, tho' I ſcorn to complain;*
*I hate and deteſt Marriage Vows to profane,*
*But his Carriage would tempt one to follow him.*

*Bel.* Nay, Madam, it muſt be own'd a Temptation, yet I know your good Senſe will carry you above it, and I am ſtill in Hopes, that Affairs will be brought to a happy Concluſion: But we are forgetting the main Buſineſs. *Mally,* my Dear, have you got every Thing in Readineſs for the Reception of your Gueſt?

*Mal.* Ay, ay, Madam, I warrant you for that, and I fancy it is juſt about the Time; for I hear *Tom* very buſy with the Servants, in the other End of the Lodging; but I muſt be gone to my Poſt at the Gate, where I am to meet Mr. *Rover,* to direct him the wrong Way, and whenever I have done that, I'll be with you immediately.    [*Exit.*

*La. Care.* Well, let's be gone to our Poſts, and wait the Event in the next Room, for I imagine the Affair is juſt at Hand.    [*Exeunt.*

SCENE VI.   Cook, Butler, Coachman, *and* Tom, *ſtanding beſide the Cheſt.*

*Butl.* Od, I have ſtrong Curioſity to know what is in it.
*Coach.* And I too.   Come, we'll break it up.
*Tom.* Hold, hold——Man, prithee don't talk ſo loud—— No, no, we muſt not break it up, leſt perhaps Sir *Robert* ſhould diſcover it; but I have a Gamlet in my Pocket, we'll bore a Hole, and look in and ſee.
*Omnes.* Ay, that will do beſt.

[*Tom bores, Sir* Robert *ſhifts.*
*Tom.* Bleſs us, the Devil is in the Cheſt.
*Coach.* Faith, I did hear ſomething move. But what has the Devil to do in our Houſe? No, no, it muſt be Thieves
designing

defigning to rob us, and they have fent one of their Number, concealed in this Cheft, to watch till we are all afleep, and then to come out, and open the Doors to the reft.

*Tom.* Indeed, *Nathaniel,* I believe you have guefs'd it; but however, that we fhould be guilty of no Miftake, I think it would be beft to watch it all Night, and, for my Part, you know I can't ftay, but I would have you three watch it Hour about, and while one watches, the other two will fleep in the next Room, to be ready at a Call.

*Coach.* It will do very well; but who fhall fit up firft?

*Butl.* Well, we'll draw Cuts who fhall do it, and I'll make them.

*Tom.* Ay, ay, that's the faireft Way.

*Butl.* Here they are——Come, draw, the fhorteft Cut fits up. [*They draw, it falls upon the* Cook.

*Tom.* Well, *Nathaniel,* you muft keep a ftrict Eye about you, and if you hear the leaft Noife, give the Alarm in a Moment.

*Butl.* Come along *Jack* —— and you can go out at the Back-Door [*To* Tom] but be fure to lock it behind you.

*Tom.* I'll warrant you for that. Well, my honeft Lads, Farewel —— If this don't do, the Devil fhall be in't. [*Afide.*
                    [*Exeunt* Tom. Coachman, *and* Butler.

*Cook.* What, are they all gone, and left me to look at the Candle. No, no, I know better Things, but if I hear the leaft Noife, I'll hollow out immediately.

[*Lyes down, and puts out the Candle. The Curtain drops.*

**SCENE VII.** *The Street before Sir* Robert's *Gate.*

*Enter* Buckram *drunk.*

                              [Buck. *fings.*

**A I R XXXII. Old Age and young.**

*I have a Wife at Home,*
  *She is turn'd fo bony,*
*A rich Knight has come*
  *To give her Gold and Money;*
        **II.**
*And for this he laid*
  *An Obligation on her,*

F                                   *When*

*Whene'er this was paid,*
  *To give him up my Honour :*
### III.
*But let him do it, if he can,*
  *I've made his Way to't thorny ;*
*Still I protest I am a Man,*
  *And my Head is noways horny.*
  Fal, dal, &c.

*Enter* Mal *from the Gate.*

*Mal.* Softly, softly, Mr. *Rover*, for the Servants are all up, and I wou'd not have it known for the World.

*Buck.* Hey-day, this is another Intrigue; I believe the whole Town are intriguing To-night, and I'm taken for Mr. *Rover*, one of the handsomest Fellows in *Edinburgh*; but since I have got Money in my Pocket, I must mind the Gentlewoman's Fee. Here Mistris, [*Gives her Money*] take this as Earnest of what you may expect.

*Mal.* Come along. Pray, Sir, let's make haste, and I will shew you the Way to my Lady's Bed-Chamber; so follow me.          [*Exeunt.*

*In the same Place enter* Rover.

*Rov.* Ha — what do I see, the Gate open ? This is prodigiously fortunate, and I hope I shall find the Way to her Bed-Chamber, but when I come there, What's to be done ? But with Opportunity and Importunity, What's not to be done ?


A I R XXXIII. Serenade. Awake thou fairest Thing, &c.

*Begone, all Fears, make Way for Pleasure ;*
  *Aid me, ye Powers, this Bliss to gain ;*
*How then, with Transports, wou'd I seize her*
  *Close in my Arms, her Lips to mine.*
### II.
*When she smiles, what killing Graces*
  *Dart from every sparkling Eye ?*
*Love and Beauty in her Face is,*
  *For her Charms Ten thousand die.*


SCENE

**SCENE IX.** *Lady* Carelefs, Belinda, *and* Buckram *following* Mally.

*Mal.* Keep off, you filly Blockhead —— What do you think I have done, Ladies, but inftead of the One I waited for, I have got fome nafty Pick-Pocket Slave —— that has put a Cheat upon me; and when I had difcovered him, he would not upon any Account be gone again? But, pray, what are you Sir? —— Who begot you, Sir? —— And what Bufinefs have you here? —— If you don't give a diftinct Account of yourfelf, let me die a Maid, you Scoundrel, if I don't pluck out your Eyes.

*Buck.* Hicup —— Demme, Madam, I'm no Taylor —— I am a Gentleman, and that you may know by my Swearing; and as for my Bufinefs here, if you pleafe to let me know the Lady who is to —— Hicup. [*A Noife without, and crying.*

*Without.* Thieves! Thieves!

*La. Care.* Ha, that muft certainly be our Cue —— What Noife is that without there?

*Without.* Thieves, Thieves, Madam, were coming to rob the Houfe, and we have catched one of them.

*La. Care.* Hold him faft, and bring him forward [*to* Belinda] it can be no other but he. Now, I hope we have him fure.

*Enter Servants with* Rover. *Whene'er they look at him they let him go.*

*La. Care. and Bel.* Ha! —— Mr. *Rover*, how's that, pray?

*Rov.* Upon my Word, Ladies, all that I have to fay is, That it was juft a Piece of Miftake, that happened by your Gate being open, and when I came in, I happened to ftumble over one of thefe Fellows in the Dark —— So they called out, Thieves, and brought me where I am —— And it has put me into fuch a Confufion, that I don't know what to fay.

*Bel.* Why, Sir, there is no Occafion for any Excufe, and the Blame is not upon you, for here is an impudent Fellow, that has not only come in at the Gate, but rudely came running into this Room, and would not be gone again, upon any Account.

*Buck.* Hicup —— upon my Soul, Mr. *Rover*, I have been a feeking you all the Town over —— to deliver your Clothes,

*and*

and now, since I have found you — you may take them.
*[Throws them off, and runs out.*

*Rov.* Poor *Buckram* has got himself drunk, and it is a very common Thing for him, upon these Occasions, to commit such Blunders : But, Ladies, I must beg the Favour of you to give the Clothes Lodging for this Night, and against To-morrow I shall do myself the Honour to wait upon you, and make my Excuse in the best Manner I can ; until then, Ladies, adieu.          *[Exit.*

*La. Care.* and *Bel.* Sir, your humble Servant. Lights there, down Stairs.

*La. Care.* But what is it that has put you all into such a Confusion this Night.          *[To the Servants.*

*Coach.* An't please your Ladyship, there is a Chest in the next Room, that was sent here this Night, under the Name of foreign Goods for Sir *Robert,* but from some Noise which we heard in it, we concluded it to be a Thief in the Chest, designing to rob the House, yet we were afraid to break it up, least it should be a Mistake, and while we watched it, this Gentleman happened to come, and being dark we took him for a Thief.

*La. Care.* Well, I commend your Diligence — but go and bring the Chest here, and we will put it out of Doubt immediately.          *[Exeunt Servants.*

*Mal.* Now I'll lay my Life upon't, that this Chest is something of *Tom's* Contrivance ; and so Ladies let us be upon our Guard.

*Enter the Servants with the Chest.*

*Butl.* An't please your Ladyship, it is very heavy. Shall we break it up ?

*La. Care.* Ay, ay, to be sure, we will see what's in it. *[They break it up,* out starts Sir Robert, *and whene'er the Servants observe him, they run out.*

*Sir.* Ha ! What do I see, in my own House kept Prisoner by my own Servants ! This is prodigiously strange.

*La. Care.* and *Bel.* Ha, ha, ha !

*Sir. Belinda* and my Wife here too, nay, then, upon my Word, Ladies, I can't stand your rallying just now. *[Exit.*

*Bel.* Ha, ha, ha ! Well, I han't been so diverted this long While. *Tom* is one of the rarest Fellows that ever I knew. Dost know where he is, *Mally ?* 'Twere a Pity not to let him know the Success.

*Mal.*

*Mal.* Yes, yes, Madam, I have him conceal'd in a little Room below Stairs. Do you think that all this could have been managed without me. *Tom, Tom,* come out of your Hole. [*Calls at the Door*] He will be here in an Inftant, Madam. O, he's coming.

*La. Care.* Well, fo far nothing could have happened better. But here comes the Contriver.

### Enter Tom.

*Tom.* Now, Ladies, I wifh you Joy, for I have overheard every Thing that has been done, and my Brain is pregnant with fome Things which I expect to accomplifh e'er this Day be at an End, in a Marriage and Agreement.

*Bel.* Why, really, *Tom,* you have performed every Thing fo well, that it would be doing you Injuftice to doubt any Thing you promife ; but this is fomething fo ftrange, that I can't help enquiring into the Means how it is to be done.

*Tom.* Well, Madam, you fhall be fatisfied, before we part, as to that. But, Ladies, I muft beg Leave to ask you a Queftion, whether or not you have as much Faith to put in me, as to truft me with the managing of two Letters, one of which I would have writ from Lady *Carelefs* to Mr. *Rover,* the other from Madam *Belinda* to Sir *Robert.*

*Bel.* Nay, for my Part, fince I have gone fo far, I won't ftop at that. What do you fay, Coufin ?

*La. Care.* Ay, to be fure, we'll ftand it to the laft, now.

*Tom.* Upon my Word, Ladies, I'm glad to hear it ; and as they have both got pretty fevere Difappointments already, to give them another, while they are out of Humour, may add a great deal to our Defign of reclaiming them ; fo, if you will pleafe to withdraw into the next Room, where we will get Pen, Ink, and Paper, I'll give you an Account of my Plot.

*Bel.* With all my Heart ; and now, Coufin, lend me your Hand. [*Sings.*

AIR XXXIV. *John* come kifs me now.
*When Sol from the Weft, as a Charioteer,*
*Drives away to the Eaft with a fwift Career,*
*Then Darknefs furrounds the neighbouring Plains,*
*And alone is the Time for intriguing Defigns.*

### II.
*Some play the Lover's Part,*
*And try a cunning Art,*

*To gain the thoughtlefs Virgin's Love,*
*He vows and fwears, by all above,*
*No falfe inconftant Swain to prove.*

### III.

*But if you refign your Treafure in Store,*
*When he's drunk with Wine he calls you a Whore,*
*Then tofts up a Health, and let's them know*
*'Twas you whom he meant, and you do fo and fo.*

### IV.

**L.** Care. and Bel. *Then let us join, my Dear,*
*And of all thofe Arts beware,*
*Nor mind what flatt'ring Creatures fay,*
*By Oaths they cheat, the Fair betray,*
*But gained once they fcorn our Sway.*

### End of the Second Act.

---

# ACT III. SCENE I.

### Rover's *Lodgings.* Enter Rover.

#### Rover.

CUrfe on my Stars, am I at laft outwited by a Woman, and made the Sport and Prey of filly Slaves; nay, what was worfe, expofed to publick Shame, and with Confufion ftand with down downcaft Looks, and faintly tell them, that I was miftaken? — In what was I miftaken? What can they think or judge was my Defign? But ftill, I can't help thinking there is a Trick at the Bottom of it, and *Mally* has cheated me; if it be fo, confound the policed Jade, I'll have no more to do with her. [*Sings.*

#### AIR XXXV. Green Sleeves.

*The Lawyer tells you, cheat none fhou'd;*
*The Parfon fays, ah, be not proud;*
*The Doctor fwears, take Pills they're good;*
*But none of them do as they fay.*

II. Thut

## II.

*Thus we who boaſt of Liberty,*
*When from the Power of Beauty free,*
*We truſt ſome ſilly ſenſeleſs ſhe,*
*And ſo become her Prey.*

*Enter a* Servant *with a Letter.*

*Serv.* Sir, here is a Letter, which was deſired to be delivered to you immediately.

*Rov.* Does he wait for an Anſwer.

*Serv.* No, Sir.                                              [*Exit.*

*Rov. Reads.*

SIR,

WHEN *you look at the Subſcription, you muſt un-doubtedly be ſurpriſed to ſee me do any Thing ſo much out of Character as this. But when* Mally *informed me of the dreadful Diſappointment that happened you this laſt Night, by* Buckram *having on your Clothes, it prevail'd upon me to do ſomething in Return ; and if you will pleaſe to give yourſelf the Trouble to call at the Back-Door, within an Hour and a Half hence, there will one attend you who ſhall give me the Honour of your Company, and by that Time all ſhall be in Readineſs for your Reception. This is all from*

Edinburgh, 12th June,                    *Yours,*
Three in the Morning.                              CELIA.

Can I truſt my Eyes, and believe this is real ? Or is it the Production of an empty Brain ? —— Ha! I have it ſtill —— I ſee it, and can read it, and it muſt be ſo. Then hence, my Fears, I'll doubt no more. But let me conſider, Three o'Clock, [*looking on his Watch*] it is not much paſt it, and it is an Hour and a Half until the Time. O! 'tis Ten thouſand Years.

*Enter* Tom.

*Rov.* Well, *Tom,* have you any News?

*Tom.* None other, Sir, than Yeſterday's Challenge. I fancy, Sir, it will be Time we were preparing, for I have my two Champions to ſeek out yet.

*Rov.* Well, *Tom,* I have juſt an Hour lyes heavy upon

my

my Hands ; and as I am obliged in Honour to attend him, I don't care much tho' I do spend it that Way.

*Tom.* Then, Sir, if you please, I'll be gone, and get all Things in Readiness — You know the Time exactly.

*Rov.* I'll attend you to an Instant, [*Exit* Tom] and this Affair, I hope, will divert me a little, till these tedious Moments are at an End. [*Sings.*

AIR XXXVI. I'll range around the Shady Bowers.
*Thus when a Sailor has endur'd*
*A Storm at Sea, with Toil inur'd,*
*His Courage bold again to try,*
*Sets out to Sea, nor fears to die.*

II.
*Thus fraught with Love, to Celia's Arms*
*I'll fly, nor think, but on her Charms ;*
*If Fortune smile, then happy I,*
*If not, I'll scorn the Sex for ay.* [Exit.

SCENE II. *A Tavern, Sir* Robert *and* Trimmer, *Wine, &c.*

*Sir.* Faith, Mr. *Trimmer,* I think myself very lucky, in meeting a Friend so early, to comfort me ; for, I can tell you, I have been but indifferently treat this last Night, and so, Sir, my humble Service to you.

*Trim.* Truly, Sir, tho' I must thank you for your Compliment, there are a great many that think my Company very agreeable ; and as to your meeting me so early, I-cod, I can tell you, I had such important Affairs upon my Hand — that I could not lie a-Bed.

*Sir.* How, Sir—why, you han't been four and twenty Hours in Town yet,—and so deeply engaged already —How's that, pray, for I don't understand it ?

*Trim.* Sir, I don't design you shou'd — for I hate to vaunt of any Thing—But, to convince you of the Truth of it—you must know, that I have a Lady's Reputation upon my Hands this Morning, which I am to vindicate, by exposing my naked Body to the Point of a drawn Sword—and immediately after I have conquer'd him, I have an Appointment with a fine polite Lady, who hath sent me this Letter, which [*Gives him a Letter*] I am so
much

much pleas'd with, that fince fhe lov'd me at firft Sight,
I defign to return her Favour, *alamode de France*, and
marry her at firft Sight.

*Sir.* But how do you know but fhe may be a Cheat?

*Trim.* No, no, Sir; I han't the leaft Apprehenfion of
that, for I am convinc'd that a Lady of fuch a fine Tafte
can never be a Cheat, and it is in vain to perfwade me
to the contrary, for I'm refolv'd upon't.

*Sir.* Nay, Sir, I affure you I have no Plot in that at
all.

### Enter a Servant.

*Serv.* Here is a Letter for you, Sir.    [*To Sir* Robert.

*Trim.* Did you look at the Direction? For I fancy it is
to me.

*Serv.* If your Name is Sir *Robert Carelefs*, it is, Sir.

*Trim.* No, no, Mr. *Andrew Trimmer* is my Name.

[*Sir* Robert *reads afide*.

SIR,

*YOU can't imagine how it vex'd me, to fee you put to
fo much Trouble this laft Night, when I was fo foolifh as to
imagine it might perhaps be upon my Account, and that you
had conceal'd yourfelf in the Cheft, on Purpofe to have an
Opportunity with me, after all was afleep. This, Sir, I affure you, has given me a great Deal of Uneafinefs, and
will never be at Reft until I have the Happinefs of feeing
you in the Chamber where I commonly fleep, at your Houfe,
againft half an Hour after fix, at which Time every Ob-
ftacle in your Way fhall be remov'd, and you fhall find an
eafy, kind, and dark Reception. This is all from,*

Yours, BELINDA.

P. S. *The Shutters of the Windows are all clofe.*

Edinburgh, June 12.
3 in the Morning.

Surprifingly ftrange — by Heaven it ftuns me, and nothing wou'd convince me it was fhe, if I did not know
her Hand as well as I do my own — But let me confider
more deliberately upon the Affair — Faith, Mr. *Trimmer*,

G                                          I was

I was defigned to have ftay'd for an Hour, or fo, and taken a Glafs with you, but there is fomething in this Letter which calls for immediate Attendance, and I hope you will excufe me.

*Trim.* Nay, Sir, you are very welcome; for I cou'd not ftay above five Minutes longer myfelf; and fo, Sir, pleafe to take your Glafs, and let's be gone.

*Sir.* With all my Heart, Sir. Succefs to us both.
[*Drinks.*

*Trim.* [*Throws down Money*] Will you pleafe to walk, Sir?

*Sir.* Pooh—hang Ceremony among Friends. [*Exeunt.*

SCENE III. *The Street.* Buckram *meeting* Tom *and* Trimmer.

*Buck.* Gentlemen, well met —— Well, are we to go about this Affair? I hate this tedious waiting. Why, I have kill'd half a Score in lefs Time. But where is my Armour? For I can't fight unlefs I be dreft like a Hero, becaufe I always behave like one—Where is't, I fay?

*Tom.* Juft at Hand here. Bring forward the Armour, Friend. Come, Mr. *Buckram*, and I'll equip you.
[*Dreffes him in Armour.*

*Buck.* Ay, with all my Heart. Sir, it is a Drefs that becomes me very much; every Body allows that—Faith, this Coat, methinks, does very well; and for the Sword, it is an incomparable good one.

*Trim.* Sir, I can promife upon the Sword. But will you pleafe to draw it, and look at it.

*Buck.* Draw it, Sir —— What, do you think I can't judge of a Sword without drawing of it?——I find you don't know me, Sir; for I have fo much Practice of Swords, that I can tell you exactly a good or bad Sword, by looking at its Scabbard.

*Trim.* Sir, I beg your Excufe; it is juft my Ignorance in the Thing.

*Tom.* Ah, Sir, he's a ftrange Fellow. But how do you like yourfelf now, Mr. *Buckram?*

*Buck.* Now, Sir, I'm a King, and my Perfon is facred; for I dare any Man to touch it. [*Struts about*] But pray, Gentlemen, before we proceed any further, let me
**know**

know the Conditions of the Fight, and how many Men are to be murder'd.

*Tom.* That I will; but you muſt take Care to commit no Murder, there is only one Fellow whom we deſign ſhou'd be deſperately hurt; but pray, Mr. *Buckram,* I beg of you to ſave his Life, poor Fellow; don't kill him altogether.

*Buck.* Why, Sir, if I be to engage with but one at a Time, I cannot promiſe; but I'll do what I can to oblige a Friend.

*Tom.* Well, that's very kind; but I hope he ſhan't come within the Reach of your Sword; for I expect Mr. *Trimmer* ſhall put him to Flight. But what I think wou'd be the beſt Way of proceeding, is, that we ſhou'd all go to the Place a little before the Time, and Mr. *Buckram* ſhall conceal himſelf upon one Side of you, and myſelf upon the other, ſo that you ſhall courageouſly appear in the Field alone —— for, I really believe, if any of them were to ſee Mr. *Buckram,* they wou'd run away, and then you ſhou'd not have the Honour of drubbing him.

*Trim.* I love the Propoſal very much; but, if you pleaſe, Sir, I incline that Mr. *Buckram* ſhou'd be exceedingly near, leaſt perhaps the Fellow ſhou'd take it in his Head to engage, and then, you know, I can ſhift a little Bit of Ground, and touch him——and then——

*Buck.* And then——
> I, *like a hungry Lyon to his Prey,*
> *Will riſe and tear him; but let's haſte away.* [Exeunt.

## SCENE IV. Lady *Careleſs, Belinda* and *Mal.*

*Bel.* Did *Tom* let you know the Means how this was to be done?

*Mal.* Yes, Madam, that I am thoroughly inſtructed in; and I'll warrant you it ſhall be manag'd well enough; never trouble yourſelf to enquire into the Means, but wait with Patience until you ſee the Event, and then we will tell you the Manner how it was effected.

*Bel.* Well, Couſin, all that I ſhall ſay, is, Heaven proſper us, poor deſperate Wretches——for to be ſure this is a deſperate Attempt——and if you pleaſe, my Dear, ſince

we have a few spare Moments, we'll divert ourselves with
a Song.

L. *Care.* With all my Heart, and then we'll begone to
our Closet.                                    [*Bel. sings.*

### AIR XXXVII. Miss *Lenoe*'s Minuet.

*Why does he fly me, when I love,*
 *And love him with a fond Desire;*
*If he doubts my Passion, let him prove*
 *My Heart sincere, and all on Fire.*

#### II.

*In my Breast, see how I'm prest,*
 *Can find no Rest,*
*Till of the wish'd for Joys possest,*
*Tell me, ye Powers, then shall I be so blest?*

#### III.

*Is't because I love you, that you scorn,*
*And leave my Heart to sigh and mourn;*
*If you are determined to disdain,*
*And take a Pleasure in giving Pain,*

#### IV.

*Love sure, is blind; for now I find*
 *That your Mind*
*Is not, by half, so sweet and kind*
*As I expected it to find.*

Come, Cousin, let's away; and, *Mally,* be upon your Guard.

*Mal.* Yes, Madam, I'll warrant you for that; and if I
don't manage it handsomly, I'll henceforth quit my Skill
in any Thing of Intrigue.                      [*Exeunt.*

### SCENE V. *The Duke's Walk,* Trimmer, Tom *and* Buckram, *as before.*

*Tom.* Now, Gentlemen, let us make all Haste to place
ourselves in Battle Array; for it is the Time appointed,
almost to an Instant, and the Enemy will be upon us.

*Buck.* Lord, how I tremble —but, Mr. *Thomas,* I hope
there is no Danger.                            [*Aside.*

*Tom.* Never fear, *Sandy* — stand it out bravely to the
last; and take my Word you shan't receive any Harm.

          [*Aside.*
          *Buck.*

*Buck.* Nay, then, Mum for that. [*To* Trimmer] Say, Mr. *Trimmer*, what Wing of the Army am I to engage?——For there is nothing like being in one's Place a little before the Time.

*Trim.* Exactly five Yards behind me——there you must ly down close to the Ground, so that, if I shou'd happen to have Occasion for you, I may retire for a Step or two, and give you the Touch; and then, Sir, you know what's to be done.

*Buck.* And then, Sir —— I shall ly flat to the Ground [*Aside*] then indeed, Sir, I know what's to be done. But come, let's to our Places. [Buck. *and* Tom *ly down.*

*Trim.* That's well done, my Lads; and yonder I see the Heiress upon the Rocks, at a Distance, to be Witness of our Victory.

*Buck.* [*Starts.*] Ha —— what Noise is that? —— Let me come at him.

*Trim.* Pray, Sir, be easy; it was nothing but a Frog that leapt into the Ditch.

*Buck.* Was it so, Sir? —— Upon my Word I thought it had been a Man in Armour. [*Lies close again.*

*Tom.* But here comes our Antagonist, and all alone too. Now, Mr. *Trimmer*, I think we have him.

*Trim.* Yes, yes, you shall see how courageously I will behave——but, Mr. *Buckram*, you must be sure to ly close, and let me have the Honour of drubbing him.

*Buck.* I'll warrant you for that, Sir. [*Lying flat*] If I don't ly close, the Blame shall be upon me.

### Rover *and* Trimmer *meet.*

*Tom.* Now, here they meet, and I think my Part of it is over; so now I'll be gone about the rest of my Business. [*Exit* Tom.

*Trim.* Sir, you are an impertinent saucy Scoundrel, to take upon you to affront any young Lady in my Company, and I design to run you throw the Guts for it. How do you love that, Sir—eh?

*Rov.* Give over your Blustering, Coxcomb, and draw your Sword.

*Trim.* Draw my Sword, Sir —— What, do you think I can't draw my Sword, Sir? [*Retiring back, puts his Foot upon* Buck. *he never moves.*] Sir, it is well known, that I have

drawn

drawn my Sword, very often [*Puts still upon* Buckram] and—

*Rov.* No more of your Words, Sir, but draw your Sword quickly, or I'll run you throw the Body. [*Trimmer endea-*
*vouring to draw.*

*Trim.* Pray, Sir, excuse me a little, for my Sword won't draw just now — but since it has happened so— here is a Man [*Points to* Buck.] who knows my Courage, and will assert it to the last Drop of his Blood—Rise, my Friend, —pray assist me to raise him; for I fancy he has fall'n asleep.

*Rov.* [*Puts up his Sword, and kicks him.*] Get out, you insignificant Fellow; it is such cowardly blustering Rascals, as you are, who impose upon Mankind — But let me see whom he has got here — I fancy just such another Coward as himself. [*Raises* Buck.] Ha, ha, *Sandy Buckram* in Armour!

*Buck.* Yes, Faith, Mr. *Rover*, it is so—but I can tell you, if I had known it had been you, I shou'd not have been so afraid of myself; but he is a sly Fellow, *Tom*; he did not tell me that; he only said, it was one of his Acquaintance.

*Trim.* —— What, Mr. *Buckram*, won't you revenge my Affront?

*Buck.* Revenge your Affront—Lord help your silly Head —and now, after the Jest is over, pray, Sir, give yourself the Satisfaction to take a full Survey of my Face, without my Steel Cap, [*Throws it off*] and see if you can't discover as great a Coward as yourself.

*Trim.* Troth, Friend, I find I am very much mistaken, for you have the Face of a down-right Coward.

*Buck.* [*In a Fury puts his Hand to his Sword*] —— Wounds, Sir—that's a Lie; for I am a Man of Courage, and if you don't be gone in an Instant, Sir ——

*Trim.* Olo, I ask your Pardon; and you are a Man of Courage, to be sure. So your humble Servant. [*Exit hastily.*

*Rov.* Well done, *Buckram*, that's like a brave Fellow; you can be a Man of Courage, upon Occasion, I see.

*Buck.* Yes, Sir —— a Coward, to a Man of Courage, may some Times prove a Man of Courage to a Coward.

*Rov.* It some Times happens so, indeed —— but I must mind Affairs of more Consequence. Adieu. [*Exit* Rov.
*Buck.*

*Buck.* What! are they all gone, and left me the sole Conqueror of the Field ? then I think it is high Time to look at the Sword—— that has gained me the Victory. [*draws it*] —— Softly —— ah, it is a dangerous Weapon; and it is a surprising Thing to me, that one Christian should have the Heart to strike another with it —— so long as I am Master of it, it shall do no harm.

### AIR XXXVIII. What tho' they call me, &c.

*Let Heroes of their fighting boast,*
*And vaunt of —— who have murder'd most;*
*But where I've fought, no Lives are lost,*
*Not one of them hurt in the Fray.*

#### II.

*Just as a Lady, drest with Art,*
*Shouts from her Eyes a killing Dart,*
*So I with Looks would pierce the Heart;*
*But none of your fighting, I pray.*

*Enter* Heiress, *in a Cloak and Hood, hastily.* Buckram *drops the Sword, she seizes it, and comes briskly up to him.*

*Heir.* Quickly tell me, Sirrah, how you have dispos'd of that insignificant Fellow, who put me to the Trouble of coming out so early this Morning to see myself affronted, by having such a cowardly Rascal to espouse my Quarrel ? Say, in an Instant, where does he ly conceal'd, or by Heavens this Sword shall be your Murderer ?

*Buck.* [*kneeling*] Pray, Madam, have Mercy, and don't —— murder a poor innocent Man, and I shall tell you all that I know of the Matter.

*Heir.* Haste then, Sirrah —— Where is he, I say ?

*Buck.* Why, he is —— But you have put me into such a Confusion —— upon my Soul I don't where he is.

*Heir.* Still trifling —— the Truth immediately, Sir, or ——

*Buck.* Olo —— Well then, if it must be so, —— as the last Words of a poor dying Man —— All that I know of the Matter is, that, upon my Soul, he's run away.

*Heir.* And this is the Truth, as you hope for Mercy.

*Buck.* As I hope for Mercy.

*Heir.* Well then, rise —— I am satisfied of your Innocence, look up brisk, now —— for I design to confer a Piece of Honour upon you.

*Buck.*

*Buck.* Honour upon me, did you fay, Madam ? Faith, with all my Heart, and no Man fhall ferve you more faithfully.

*Heir.* Well, I fee you are an honeft Fellow, and a little skill'd in Intrigue —— Therefore I will truft you —— but anfwer me one Queftion, Could you play the Part of a Waiting-Maid, if you were dreft accordingly ?

*Buck.* Ay, that I can, Madam, to a Nicety.

*Heir.* Well, then, follow me. [*Exeunt.*

## SCENE VI. *The Street, at Sir* Robert's *Gate.* Enter Jean *and* Tom.

*Tom.* Lookye, now, the Door is open, and if you don't find him in that Houfe, I'll be hang'd.

*Jean.* And if I don't fearch for him, I fhall be hang'd. [*Exeunt.*

*Tom.* Well done, *Tom* —— Now I think this is all that I have to do in this Plot, and if the Ladies don't play their Parts, upon themfelves be the Blame. But as to my other Affair —— Ha, ha, ha ! as I live I fhall die with Laughing, to think how I fhall perfonate the travell'd Beau —— *Morbleu,* Madamofelle fhall find me an Abridgment of all the *Gens de goût,* that has appeared in *France* or *Spain* thefe hundred Years. By *Jupiter,* fhe won't hold out Half a Second —— I'll ply her fo with the tender, the paffionate, and the brisk Gallant too, if there fhould be Occafion for it, along with the reft of the Artillery of Love, that if fhe does not furrender at firft Interview, I'll be hung by the Neck like a Dog. But I muft about it immediately. [*Exit.*

## SCENE VII. *A Chamber in Sir* Robert's *Houfe.* Enter Jean *in at the Door of a Room,* Mally *follows her foftly.*

*Mal.* Now, I think I have her fure enough —— but I muft watch the Back-Door, for 'tis the Time to a Minute. [*Exit.*
*Locks the Door.*

*Jean.* There is nothing in this Houfe, I believe, but Darknefs and Silence ; the Shutters of the Windows are fo clofe, that you fhall fcarcely know whether it is Daylight or not ; the Doors are all open, and not the Stir of a Moufe to be heard : But if I fhould find that drunken Slave
fleeping

sleeping in any Corner of it, with my dear, dear twenty Guineas, I should think my Pains all well bestowed.

*Enter* Mally *introducing Mr.* Rover.

*Mal.* You'll find my Lady in this Room, and I'll take Care that you shan't have the least Alarm from Sir *Robert* —your humble Servant. [*Exit* Mal.

*Jean.* Ha! what's this I hear? Pray Heaven she ben't in this Room; and since I have lost the Knight, I'll personate his Lady. [*Aside.*

*Rover.* Pray, Madam, be so kind as to let me know where you are.

*Jean.* Sir, I'm afraid you have lost your Way. [*He catches her in his Arms.*

*Rov.* No——for here I've found it. O, let me press you to my burning Breast, and breathe my Soul away beneath your Feet.

*Enter La.* Care. Bel. *and* Mal. *with Lights. All laugh.* Jean *runs out.*

*Bel.* Heavens protect me, Mr. *Rover* in the Embraces of a Strumpet!

*Rov.* Indeed, Ladies —— I am so thunderstruck, that I scarcely know where I am: But, Lady *Careless*, a Word with you, if you please.

*L. C.* With all my Heart, Sir. [Rov. *and* L. Care. *aside.*

*Rov.* I fancy, Madam, 'tis almost needless to ask you if you know the Owner of this Letter? [*Shows her the Letter.*

*L. C.* Well, Mr. *Rover*, to deal honestly with you, I do know the Author of the Letter, as also of every Thing else that has happened you this last Night; but when you know, that the whole Design was intending your Happiness, I hope you'll judge favourably of our Behaviour.

*Rov.* Madam, every Thing, at present, appears to me so like a Riddle, that unless it be explained, I shall never be able to form any Judgment of the Matter.

*L. C.* Then, Sir, to be plain, my Cousin *Belinda*——has entertain'd a Passion for you, a considerable Time; and as long as you continued in that fickle, inconstant Humour, she could never have the smallest Hopes, and in order to give you a Distaste of this rambling Course of Life, we fix'd upon this Night to put our Designs in Execution; this is the whole unravelling of the Affair; and as we have an entire Confi-

H                                                                    dence

dence in your good Senfe, we have left it altogether in your Power, to make what Interpretation you pleafe.

*Rov.* Well, Madam, your generous Declaration has fo great an Effect upon me, that if this Lady [*kneels to Bel.*] can overlook the paft Folies of my Life, whatever is in my Power, for the future, fhall be entirely devoted to her Service.

*Bel.* Rife, Sir, for my unwary Conduct, in this Affair, makes that Pofture rather become me than you; but as I have all along entertained fuch a Notion of you, that I know nothing with which I cou'd not truft you, fo now I'll never fcruple putting myfelf wholly into your Power; yet I own I have been very foolifh.

*Rov.* [*Catching her in his Arms.*] Generous Creature! By Heavens, that Confeffion makes me the happieft of Mankind.

*L. C.* Now, *Belinda*, fince this Conclufion is fo happy, it gives me good Hopes of the other; and, Sir, this is an Affair in which we beg the Favour of your Affiftance.

*Rov.* Whatever is in my Power, Ladies, you need not doubt, is at your Service.

*Bel.* Then, Sir, if you pleafe to withdraw into the other Apartment, we'll open the whole Affair to you.

*Rov.* With all my Heart, Madam, and now,

> *Let Virtue ftill be call'd a foolifh Thought,*
> *And pleafing Vice, with dear Experience bought,*
> *I found 'mongft all its Charms that fill'd my Breaft,*
> *Its Pleafures vainly rob'd me of my Reft,*
> *And all its Joys are trifling at the beft.*

**SCENE VIII.** *Difcovers the Heirefs at a Glafs and* Buck. *behind her, dreft as a Lady's Gentlewoman.*

*Heir.* Betty——Betty, my Dear, does not think I look charmingly to Day, Child?

*Buck.* [*Aping a Woman*] O, yes, Madam, inchantingly fine——but——but, Madam, if you pleafe, I don't like *Betty* for a Name, I'd rather have fome fine Romantick Name —— fuch as —— *Ifabella*——that's a fine Name, now; but *Betty* is a Whore's Name.

*Heir.*

*Heir. Betty*, a Whore's Name—Sirrah, you Rafcal, have a Care—for it is my Name, and it is a fine one, and I like to hear it.

*Buck.* Lord—Madam, I had forgot, it was not *Betty*, I meant; for, I muft own, *Betty* is a very fine Name—But, Madam, I hope you have difpofed of your Gentlewoman, for if fhe interfere in the Plot, fhe may fpoil all.

*Heir.* Ay, ay, fhe is fafe enough, I warrant you, for fhe has the moft unlucky Hand in an Intrigue of any that ever tried it—fhe has affronted me above half a dozen Times already, but I have taken Care that fhe fhan't be engag'd in this—but don't you think, *Betty*, that I fhall be prodigioufly happy in fuch a fine Gentleman?

*Buck.* Yes, yes,—Madam, to be fure—but you have not feen him yet, Have you?

*Heir.* Seen him—that's true. I han't feen him; but, in my Opinion, it was impoffible, that any, but one of an extraordinary fine Tafte, cou'd write fuch a handfom Letter as, I fhew'd you, he has fent me—and then it is fo *alamode*, that if he comes, in any Meafure, up to the Idea I have form'd of him, I'm refolv'd to marry him at firft Meeting, according to the Propofal.

*Buck.* That will be *alamode*, indeed, Madam, and then, being fo foon in the Morning—But don't you defign to examine a little into his Character; for, perhaps, he may be a Cheat?

*Heir.* Ay, but the Letter—the Letter—fuch a fine Letter; you had forgot that, I fancy.

*Buck.* Olo—yes, Faith, Madam, I did forget that. But hark, fome Body comes.

*Enter a Servant.*

*Serv.* Madam, there is a fine brisk Beau, who defires to know if her Ladyfhips, the Heirefs, be at Leifure this Morning.

*Heir. Betty*, hafte and conduct him in. [*Exit Buck. and Servant*] Her Ladyfhip, the Heirefs! Ay, to be fure, it muft be he. Well, thofe travell'd Gentlemen are the beft manner'd People in the World—They have fuch inviting Ways of fpeaking, one might live a thoufand Years before they wou'd have fuch a kind Expreffion from a home-bred Fellow—But here he comes.

*Enter*

*Enter* Buck. *introducing* Tom *dreſt as a travell'd Beau.*

*Tom.* Pardon me, celebrated Beauty, for daring, ſo *mal a propos*——Ha! thunderſtruck by the *Eclat* of her Charms ——Madam, by your innumerable Perfections —— I was never in ſuch a Confuſion in my Life —— Thoſe Eyes have beheld all the fine Women *Europe* can boaſt of, yet did I never feel half the Emotion your Ladyſhip has occaſioned in my Breaſt——Pray, Madam, does your Ladyſhip chuſe *Rapee* or plain *Spaniſh?* they are both at your Service, I aſſure you; and for their Goodneſs, *Madam la Ducheſs de Bourgogne* ſhall anſwer for the one, and the *Spaniſh* Ambaſſador the other, from whom I had them.

*Heir.* [*Aſide*] What a Prodigy of Gallantry he is! [*to him*] Pray, Sir, which of them is uſed moſt in foreign Courts, at preſent?

*Tom.* The *Rapee,* Madam.

*Heir.* Then that ſhall determine me. Is this it, Sir?
                [*Takes the Box, and takes a Pinch and returns it.*

*Tom.* Yes, Madam, the beſt ever *America* produc'd.

*Heir.* I need not ask you, if you have been in *France,* or that you have ſeen the Manners of that politeſt of Nations? Your Air ſufficiently diſcovers it to all Beholders.

*Tom.* I muſt own, Madam, I retain a good deal of the Manners and Carriage, *que tout le Monde* ſo juſtly admire in the *French.* I have been, Madam, in Company of all the fineſt People in *Paris,* of both Sexes——The Ladies cou'd never want me from the Head of the Dance, nor the Gentlemen from the Head of the Table. Neither is *France* the only Place where I have ſhone at the Head of the *Gens d'Eſprit; Italy, Germany, Spain, Savoy,* have all confeſt that there is ſomething very extraordinary about me.

*Heir.* Really, Sir, it needs ſurprize no Body that you have been ſo well received every where; and I muſt confeſs you far excel all the Travellers I have ſeen, in fine Improvements.

*Tom. Ma foy, Madam,* the greateſt Part of Travellers *ne ſont que des Ignorans.* They amuſe themſelves with the muſty Records of Antiquity, and ſtuff their Heads with a Galamatias of Obſervations on the Trade, Religion, and Government of the Country they paſs through. *Quelle Aveuglement!* —— All mere Trifles, that become a finiſh'd

Gentle-

Gentleman as well as an unfashionable Suit of Clothes, or the Grimaces of a religious Bigot.

*Heir.* What Monster have you describ'd!——I sicken at the Narration——But, Sir, as these are Creatures below the Notice of People of a refin'd *Goût*——let us leave them, and do Justice to our illustrious Cotemporaries, who are, in my Opinion, so many blazing Luminaries, that dispel the thick Clouds of Barbarism that darken the World.

*Tom. Morbleu,* that's very fine —— why, Madam, you have given them a finer Elogium, in few Words, than the best Poets wou'd have done in whole Volumes: But now, that I am talking of Poets, you must know, that I am a great Admirer of Poetry of all Kinds, especially dramatick, such as *Cato,* or *Hobb*'s Opera—— You have, no doubt, seen, Madam, the famous new Tragedy of —— of —— but the Name, it was written by a Fellow that us'd to be glad of my Company—*Voltaire*——I helped the Fellow through most of the principal Scenes of it —— tho' it goes by his Name——but I value not the Praise of the World. I presented the *Duchess de la Vere* with an Epigram, that she was highly delighted with, on this Occasion. We were dancing together at a Ball at Court, where her Grace's Petticoats intangling her Grace's Feet, her *Grace* made a Stumble ; but I catch'd her *Grace* in my Arms, and prevented her falling ; her Grace, as a Reward of my Service, appointed me next Night at her Grace's Lodgings——Ha! what have I said ? but I did not intend to ruin the Lady's Reputation ; and besides she made me swear Secresy. The Verses were very pretty, and, I must own, took me five or six Mornings to think on them. I have, since I came thence, been at the Pains to translate them into *English,* for the Sake of the *British* Ladies, who, I make no Doubt, will give them their due Praise.

[*Sings in a ridiculous Manner.*]

> *Thrice blest be the Chance*
> *Which made my Goddess fall,*
> *In the midst of the Dance*
> *Amongst the Nobles all.*
> ## II.
> *I graspt her falling Charms*
> *Within my outstretch'd Arms,*

*Which*

*Which gave the Beaux Alarm,
And set her on equal Terms.*

This last Line, Madam, falls short of the rest in poetical Elegance, which is owing to the Barrenness of the *English* Tongue, for in the *French* it was allowed to be vastly pretty.

*Heir.* [*Aside*] How he charms me! Pray Heaven I don't say some foolish Thing, in the Condition he has put me in ——Sir, I am at a Loss to express my Admiration of your Parts and Person; your Air and Address is——

*Tom.* [*Interrupting her*] *Je vous entens bien*, Madam, you are going to repeat what all the *Belles* in *France* have often told me to no Purpose——*Mais, mon Ange*, I have a Secret to impart to you. Your irresistible Charms have, at last, subdued my Aversion to Matrimony, and, wou'd you believe it, I intend to marry you immediately.

*Heir.* Gods! What Extravagance——but I'm too hasty, when I don't know what Alterations may have happened in the Art of Love beyond Sea. Sir——the Novelty of your Declaration shocks me, and makes me very curious to know the present Method of carrying on Amours abroad.

*Tom.* Ha, ha, ha! With what Reluctance People consent to what is *alamode* and polite? Why, Madam, this is so universally practis'd amongst the *Beau Monde*, that there is no pretending to any distinguishing Qualifications without it.

*Heir.* Bless me! What a Precipice have you saved me from! Forfeit all Pretensions to any distinguishing Qualifications, and sink amongst vulgar Souls! What a Fright you put me in! But I hope you will excuse me, and not expose me for such a Piece of Rusticity.

*Tom.* Excuse you, dear Madam——that I wou'd, tho' I were no Gainer by your Repentance; but as that discovers the Agreement of our Inclinations, it wou'd be monstrous Ingratitude to expose you. *Y a-t-il au monde, un homme aussi heureux que moi? Non certainement.*

*Enter a Servant.*

*Serv.* Sir, there is a Servant at the Door, who desires to speak with you.

*Tom.* Bid him come in. [*Exit Servant*] I hope this Freedom does not, in any Measure, disoblige your Ladyship.

*Heir.*

*Heir.* Not in the leaft, Sir.

*Enter a Servant, who whispers* Tom.

*Tom.* Hafte, begone, tell them we'll wait of them in an
Inftant. [*Exit Servant*] This, Madam, is infinitely lucky.
I have a Sifter whom I intrufted with my Defign this Morning, and as fhe was fully convinc'd of my fine Accom-
plifhments, made no Doubt of the Succefs; and, being engaged after the fame Manner herfelf, has fent me Word that
fhe waits for us, with a Parfon ready to perform the Ceremony to both Parties; and as the Opportunity calls this
Inftant, I hope, Madam, you will not delay my Happinefs.

*Heir.* Ah! Sir, you have fubdu'd my Heart——for who
cou'd withftand fuch Gallantry divine? *Betty*, you muft
accompany us, my Dear.

*Buck.* Yes, Madam, [*crying*] But, dear Madam, let me
take my laft Farewel of your Virginity. [*Takes her in his
Arms, and hugs her*]——Pray, Madam, confider what you
do. Pray, Madam, don't enter rafhly into Marriage ——
Oh——

*Tom.* [*Afide*] Ha! I muft ftop this Jade's Mouth, or fhe
will fpoil all. [*Runs and puts a Guinea in* Buckram's *Mouth*]
Pray, *Betty*, have a care, you will fuffocate your Miftris.

*Buck.* [*Looking at it*] Ha! a Guinea, that was what I
wanted. [*to her*] But believe me, Madam, you will be exceedingly happy in fuch a fine Gentleman.

*Tom.* Now, Madam, lend me your Hand,

*And let's be join'd in* Hymen's *facred Tye;
We'll live in Love, and then, at length, we'll die.*
[*Exeunt.*

SCENE IX. *Sir* Robert's *Houfe. Lady* Careless *fola.*

AIR XL. The yellow hair'd Ladie.
*How vain are the Pleafures that Mankind purfue?
How empty their Wifhes, their Virtues how few?*
II.
*No Good without Danger, and all our beft Joys
Are crouded with Cares and perplexing Annoys.*

*Con-*

### III.

*Contentment alone is that Blessing of Life,*
*Which comforts the Maid, and makes happy the Wife;*
### IV.
*When Hardships befal me, to this I will fly,*
*Contented I'd live, and contented I'd die.*

Well, so far has succeeded to Admiration, which gives me very good Hopes of this; and if it do not succeed, I shall never attempt another——But here he comes.

*Enter Sir* Robert.

*Sir.* My charming inchanting Angel!—— O let me hear the Whisper of your Tongue, to lead me to that Heaven of Pleasures, that dwells upon your Bosom. [*He catches her in his Arms*] Transports and Extasies! Ten thousand Sweets are on those lovely Lips! And here I swear, by Heavens, I never was so happy. Here I could live and die with Satisfaction.

*Enter* Bel. *and* Rov. *with Lights. Both laugh.*

*Rov.* Ha —— Sir *Robert,* methinks you are a very fond Husband, indeed.

*L. C.* [*Kneels to Sir* Robert] Oh——that I did not know to whom these last Words were meant! that I cou'd be so insensible as to apply them to myself! then, then, I shou'd be happy indeed; yet I have seen it otherways——I have seen the Day, when, with Pleasure, you have gaz'd upon these now deserted Charms; but now they are become so hateful to you, I'm resolved from this Moment I shall never disturb you more.

*Sir.* [*Raises her, and takes her in his Arms*] Charming Woman! when I reflect upon my Behaviour, I cannot but be astonish'd at the ridiculous and ungenerous Returns I have made thy Love : But if asking Forgiveness, in the most submissive Manner, [*kneels*] with a Promise of eternal Constancy for the future, can, in any Measure, make Amends for my past Actions, and gain any Credit for my future, here publickly I swear to perform it.

*L. C.* Rise, Sir *Robert,* I cannot see you thus. An unexpected Turn gives me such an agreeable Surprize, that I am quite at a Loss what to say, but if you are sincere, I do not know a Woman whose Condition I would envy.

*Sir.*

# BUCKRAM *in Armour.* 65

*Sir.* Indeed, Madam, I own you have great Reason to doubt my Sincerity ; but I am so conscious of my own Ingenuity in the Affair, that I do not insist upon your forgiving me, till my future Conduct prove my Intentions.

*La. Care.* No, Sir *Robert*, I scorn a jealous Spirit, and let those incredulous Fools, that have no Trust to put in any but themselves, be deceived — but I will freely forgive every Thing — and let what is past be for ever sunk in Oblivion. Here, take my Hand, and with it my Heart, unspotted as it was when you receiv'd it upon our Wedding-Day.      [*He takes it, and embraces her.*
[She sings.

A I R XLI.   *John Hay's* bony Lassy.
*Thus Flowers sprout in Spring,*
  *After Winter's cold Chilling;*
*Thus the Birds mount and sing*
  *When the Time is of Billing;*
**II.**
*Thus the Miser exults,*
  *When he's found his lost Treasure;*
*But those faintly paint out*
  *All this Transport of Pleasure.*

*Sir.* Well, Madam, I must own myself very much indebted to your Generosity, and, as far as it lyes in my Power to make a Return, you may expect it; but [*to* Rover *and* Belinda] come forward; you shall wish us Joy.

*Rov.* With all my Heart, Sir; but you must know, that we expect to be first in Hand, tho'.

*Sir.* How's that, Mr. *Rover* — Married!

*Rov.* Yes, Sir. After mature Deliberation, I have at last resolv'd to venture upon that State, and I am in the Expectation of reaping a great deal more Satisfaction and Happiness in the Enjoyment of my charming Partner, than in all the World besides.

*Sir.* Joy, then, to you both; and I wish you Health and Happiness.

*Rov. and Bel.* We return you Thanks, Sir.

A I R XLII.   Man of War's Minuet.

Bel.    *How delightful are the Embraces*
     *Of a Husband kindly prest.*
I
*Happy*

*Happy, with Ten thousand Blisses,*
*Is the Wife when thus caress'd.*

### II.

*None can measure, how great's the Pleasure,*
*That they enjoy when so blest ;*
*A pleasant Folly, always jolly,*
*Makes a Husband of the best.*

### III.

Rov. *What in Life is more comforting,*
*Than a Woman full of Charms ;*
*Every Moment is transporting,*
*When within a Beauty's Arms.*

### IV.

*And each Feature's design'd by Nature*
*T'adorn the heavenly Creature's Face ;*
*Straight, then, seize her, try to please her,*
*In a soft and sweet Embrace.*

*Enter a Servant.*

*Ser.* Sir, there is one Mr. *Andrew Trimmer,* who desires to know if he may have Admittance along with his
Company.

*Sir.* Desire him in.

*Enter Mr.* Trimmer, *leading in* Mally *drest as a fine Lady,*
*and* Tom *leading the Heiress,* Buckram *following, as*
*before.*

*Trim.* Gentlemen and Ladies, we are all your humble
Servants : But before you speak one Word more, you must
wish us Joy.

*Sir.* And you are all fairly join'd, you say.

*Trim.* and *Heir.* All fairly join'd, Sir, we assure you.

*Sir.* And pray, Sir, do us the Favour to let us know
who they are.

*Rov.* That will I, Sir, — Harkye, *Tom,* did you take
Care that my Boots were well clean'd, before you came
from Home ?

*Tom.* [*Bows to his Master*] Yes, Sir, that was done, I
can assure you.

*Rov. Mally,* you Gipsy, why don't you ask your Lady's Pardon for staying out so long ?

[Mally *comes to her Lady*

*Mal.* Madam, I ask your Pardon, I hope you won'
be angry.

Omnes.

*Omnes.* Ha, ha, ha!

*Sir.* Ha, ha! What, Mr. *Trimmer*, was you obliged to take such a round about Plot to marry our Gentlewoman? If you had made me privy to the Affair, you might have had her without all this Trouble.

*Trim.* Why—why, I thought she had been a fine, polite, fashionable Lady, and a great Fortune—Did not you say so, Madam?

*Mal.* Say so, Sir! Ay—and what then? Was not you a silly Fool to believe me?

*Buck.* Hey-day, What the Devil's now to do?

*Heir.* What, Sir, [*to* Tom.] Do you think, that, instead of a fine travel'd Gentleman, I am to be satisfied with a *Valet de Chambre?* — No, you Rogue, I'll spend the one Half of my Fortune at the Law, to have you ruin'd —you Rascal.

*Trim.* And I have a good thousand Pound, which I can well spare—I'll join you, Madam, to get rid of my Wife too.

*Rov.* Well, Mr. *Trimmer*, wou'd not you think yourself obliged to any one who should free you without any Noise, for the one Half of the Money?

*Trim.* Yes, Faith. I'd give Five hundred Pounds, with all my Heart, to get free of it without any Noise.

*Heir.* And I, Sir, upon the same Conditions, will make up the Thousand, with Ten thousand good Wills; for if it were publickly known—I don't believe that ever I should be able to shew myself in the Assembly, or Play-House, again.

*Rov.* Well, this you both confirm, before these Witnesses, upon your Word of Honour, to perform.

*Both.* Upon our Honour to perform.

*Rov. Mally*—Now, it is your Turn to speak.

*Mal.* Yes, Sir—Since it is so, then, Gentlemen and Ladies, we must ask your Pardon for the Freedom, because it is nothing else but a mock Marriage; for the Fellow that perform'd the Ceremony is no Parson.

*Trim.* and *Heir.* — A mock Parson!

*Heir.* Indeed; and I am glad to hear it, altho' it is with the Expence of Five hundred Pounds. For what is that when compar'd with the Loss of one's Reputation?

But,

But, Gentlemen and Ladies, I hope you won't be so unmerciful as to divulge it through the Town.

*Rov.* That is just according as you both perform your Promise, in paying that Thousand Pound to *Mally* and *Tom*, whom I here give in Marriage to one another, [*gives Mally's Hand to* Tom] and this as Part of their Reward for their last Night's good Management.

*Heir.* Nay, then, if that be all the Danger, that shan't be long.

*Trim.* Yes, yes, Madam, with all my Heart, as soon as you please; for People of our Character should not risk it for such a Trifle as that; but, Gentlemen and Ladies ——

[Buckram *stops him.*

*Buck.* Pray, Mr. *Trimmer,* let's have Word about, and since you are making Discoveries, I think it is high Time that I should discover myself too. [*A Noise without, and crying*] Eho! that's my Wife's Tongue, and I'll delay it till that Noise be over —— [*without*] *Sandy Buckram —— Sandy Buckram.*

*Enter* Jean *running.*

*Jean.* Where is my Husband ?—— Where is *Sandy Buckram* ? I have lost my Husband, and he is in this House. Give me my Husband again.

*Tom.* Come, prithee, hold your Bawling. Gentlemen and Ladies, since the Affairs of this last Night are brought to such a happy Conclusion, I think it would be a Pity to allow any of our Company to go away dissatisfied; and therefore I would propose a Rectification of Matters betwixt *Sandy Buckram* and his Wife.

*Sir.* That I was thinking of before. *Sandy,* poor Fellow, has got into Disguise some Way or other, and was just about to make the Discovery, when his Wife came in —— Come forward, *Sandy,* don't be afraid, Man, and plead your own Cause.

*Buck.* Well, since I find I have so many good Friends about me, I will not be afraid, for she dare not beat me in your Honour's Company, I know; and really—— it would make your Heart sore to see how she abuses me sometimes.

*Sir.* Poor, honest, simple Fellow! Well, Mris. *Buckram,* I find you will be obliged to promise before this Company, that you will maltreat your Husband no longer; and

if

if ever after he makes a Complaint on you, I'll procure him a Divorce.

*Jean.* Really, Sir *Robert*, I have always had a Check of Conscience for doing it ; and since you desire it, I never will do it again : But he was so simple——

*Sir.* That you could not keep from beating him. But, to make Affairs more comfortable for you both, since you have been engaged in the Affairs of this last Night, I'll give you five hundred Pounds.

*Buck.* Five hundred Pounds——Come, come, *Jeany*, kiss and be Friends [*kisses her*] this will make us as merry as—— but I'll say no more till we get home, where we shall eat and drink, and so forth——

*Sir.* As I intend that this Day shall be a Day of rejoicing in my House, I'm sure, *Rover*, you will join in it ; use it as your own, else I shall take it for an unfriendly Action.

*Rov.* Sir, I thank you heartily for your kind Invitation. And now, my charming Partner, lend me your Hand.

     A I R XLIII. Madam *Violante*'s Minuet.
      *Hence, all my foolish Inclinations ;*
      *Farewell, for ever, unruly Passions ;*
               II.
       *Virtue has charm'd me,*
       *And so alarm'd me,*
       *That it has arm'd me*
         *Against every Vice.*
               III.
L. C. & B. *Since then we're freed from every perplexing Care,*
      *Let no poor Creature in Love e'er despair ;*
        *To Love be true,*
        *No Falshoods pursue,*
      *And Justice, in Time, will resign what is due.*
               IV.
*Buck.*     *But yet I tell you, that since e'er the World began,*
      *Women were Curses and Plagues unto Man.*
*Omnes.*    *They were design'd*
      *Always to be kind,*
    *But 'mongst them both Angels and Devils you'll find.*

                        E P I-

# EPILOGUE.

## By another Hand.

## Spoken by Mrs. *WOODWARD.*

*Gallants, in humble Strain, from Bays I'm come
To take your Plaudits, or receive his Doom.
'Tis the first Fault, be tender in your Sentence;
Gentle Rebukes may work to true Repentance.
Errors in Youth you'll easily forgive,
Since it as nat'ral is to sin, as live.
But one Excuse, in Justice, may be made
For our young Dabbler in the scribbling Trade,
With Pain he sees the Muse neglected here,
Shunning to charm, nor daring to appear,
As if not born t' inspire his native Land,
But feeding us with Wit at second Hand.
Shall Caledonians thus to others bend,
And on the Bounty of their Muse depend;
O'er the known World who greater have appear'd?
In Armies follow'd, honour'd, and rever'd?
Firm to their Friends, and by their Foes much fear'd?
In Councils awful, nor in Courts less bright;
Esteem'd of Men——of Ladies the Delight.
Exert yourselves to wipe off the Disgrace,
Nor hold in Poetry a second Place.
This is the Motive that inspir'd young Bays,
Who pleads no Merit, looks for little Praise.
Let him be only kindly understood;
If nothing else, sure the Design is good.
Pray let that move you in the Stripling's Cause,
To crown his Infant-Labours with Applause.*

## F I N I S.

A

# New SONG,

## HUMBLY DEDICATED

### TO THE

## Society of *Free-Mafons*.

Set to Mufick by a Brother of that Honourable FRATERNITY; but as there are no
Types in any of the Printing-Houfes
here, for Mufick, we are obliged to re-
fer you to the common Ball-Mufick in
Town, where Copies of the Tune may
be had; as alfo of the other one fet by
*Matthew Briggs.*

ATtend, ye Sons of ancient Fame,
  All who can vaunt the glorious Name,
Of Mafon free,
For this fhall be
A lafting and immortal Theme.
### II.
Was ever heard a Tale fo rare,
A Secret kept with fo much Care;
  To Thoufands known,
  Yet all muft own,
'Twas never breath'd in common Air.

### III.

But see, the Vulgar stand amaz'd,
And swallow what some Fool has blaz'd;
   The idle Dreams,
   The empty Whims
Of some lunatick Fellow craz'd.

### IV.

Thus Fools, while in a mortal State,
Pry in to view the Books of Fate;
   But none alive,
   And still survive,
Our awful Horrors dare relate.

### V.

Then let us join our Notes and sing,
With Voices make the Lodge to ring,
   We'll dance around
   The magick Ground,
From whence our sacred Word doth spring.

### VI.

And while the wond'ring World admire,
What secret Powers our Souls inspire,
   Thro' Time to come
   Its Praise shall run,
And last as Sol's eternal Fire.

## A DREAM.

To the Tune of, Fany blooming fair.

Last Night, when Cynthia's Beams
   Supply'd Sol's golden Ray,
While, round us, in our Dreams,
   The wanton Spirits play,

### II.

Some kind propitious Power,
   A Nymph, all o'er with Charms,
My guardian Angel, sure,
   Convey'd into my Arms.

### III.

I trembling stood and gaz'd,
   While in her sparkling Eyes
Love's flaming Chariot blaz'd,
   My Soul was all Surprize,

IV. Afrai

#### IV.

*Afraid to speak or move,*
  *Till thus she seem'd to say,*
*Indulge your growing Love;*
  *Fear nothing, but obey.*

#### V.

*Thus, by her Smiles inspir'd,*
  *Like Lightning in a Storm,*
*Swift, all on Raptures fir'd,*
  *I seiz'd the charming Form.*

#### VI.

*O Heavens! how heavenly blest!*
  *What Extasies divine*
*I felt, while thus I prest*
  *Her lovely Lips to mine!*

## A SONG.

To the Tune of, *She rose and let me in.*

*When first I saw my Charmer's Face,*
  *My Heart was flight'ring fain;*
*The Hills and Dales, thro' every Place,*
  *Her Praise I made proclaim.*

#### II.

*How some Times, as it were by Chance,*
  *Her Eyes, bright as the Day,*
*Wou'd cast a kind bewitching Glance,*
  *With such commanding Sway,*

#### III.

*That oft I wish'd myself a Stone,*
  *Quite senseless of those Charms;*
*Some Thing that cou'd not sigh and moan,*
  *Or else in Celia's Arms.*

#### IV.

*Ye Gods! cou'd I attain this Bliss,*
  *What more wou'd I desire?*
*My ravish'd Soul, at every Kiss,*
  *Wou'd faint and half expire.*

K                                    A SONG

# A SONG

## To the Tune of, *Down, down, &c.*

'Tis known to wife Sages, who judge of the Mind,
Who try every Action, and wherefore defign'd,
That Self-love and Pleafure determine Mankind
    To a Down, down, &c.

### II.

The Parfon, when preaching up Heaven's great Joy,
Muft threaten the Blacknefs of Hell to deftroy;
That Blacknefs relates to the black little Toy,
    Or a Down, down, &c.

### III.

The Lawyer, when ftudying a Speech for the Bar,
For Law-Suits in Peace, or for Tumults in War,
He thinks of a Skirmifh with Mifs, if he dare
    Lay her down, down, &c.

### IV.

The Doctor, fo famous for Knowledge and Skill,
When judging a Cafe, or prefcribing a Pill,
Their Ufe is, perhaps, for a Something that's ill,
    Or a Down, down, &c.

### V.

The Soldier in Battle, all full of Defire
For Honour, behold him, his Conduct admire,
He cocks up his Firelock, but wou'd let loofe his Fire
    In a Down, down, &c.

### VI.

The Merchant, when all his fine Goods are prepar'd,
For Sale, then he handfomly ufes his Yard;
But this makes him think of a pleafant Reward
    In a Down, down, &c.

### VII.

'Mongft Sailors, the deep Seas the fafeft are found,
But by Rocks and quick Sands there have many bee
   drown'd,
Yet move where you pleafe, there is no finding Ground
    In a Down, down, &c.

### VIII.

But that to all Parties I may give their Due,
The Ladies, when young, are all learning to few;
While ftitching, they wifh they were ufed fo too,
    Or down, down, &c.

*F I N I S.*

The Philosopher's Opera

*Bibliographical note:*
*This facsimile has been made from a copy in the*
*Henry E. Huntington Library*
*(131018)*

# T H E

# P H I L O S O P H E R's

# O P E R A.

*E tenebris tantis tam clarum extollere lumen*
*Qui primus potuisti, illustrans commoda vitæ,*
*Te sequor, O Graiæ gentis decus, inque tuis nunc*
*Fixa pedum pono pressis vestigia signis.*    Lucret.

[Price Four Pence.]

# DRAMATIS PERSONÆ.

As it ought to be reprefented at *Edinburgh*.

| | |
|---|---|
| SATAN. | *Mr* Digges. |
| SULPHUREO, } *Devils.* | *Mr* Ryder. |
| APOLLYO, | *Mr* Duncomb. |
| *Mr* GENIUS. | *Mr* Love. |
| *Mr* MORAL SENSE. | *Mr* Lancafhire. |
| *The Rev. Mr* MASK. | *Mr* Heyman. |
| JACKY. | *Mr* Younger. |

## W O M E N.

| | |
|---|---|
| *Mrs* SARAH PRESBYTERY, *relict of Mr* John Calvin. } | *Mr* Stamper. |
| ANNE, *her waiting-woman.* | *Mrs* Davenport. |
| *Mifs* SPRIGHTLY. | *Mifs* Ryder. |
| *Mifs* WEEPWELL. | *Mrs* Love. |
| *Mifs* SOB. | *Mrs* Stamper. |
| *Mifs* PITY. | *Mrs* Hopkins. |
| *Mifs* BLUBBER. | *Mrs* Salmon. |
| MOLL KITCHEN. | *Mrs* Ward. |

# TO

# The READER.

IN the Dramatis Personæ of this opera, there are two characters, and but two, which are not imaginary. Before you pronounce it wrong to point out two men now
living, you would do well to consider the scurrilous terms
in which they have pointed out two men long since dead and
gone. Remember the barbarism of Shakespear, the licentiousness of Otway, and that the author of DOUGLAS has
been preferred to both. If (as a late writer will have it)
the use of ridicule is " not to investigate known truth, but
" to expose known falsehood," it is surely as properly employed against the man who avers, that DOUGLAS is a
faultless play, as it was against the hair-brained knight-er-
rant, who maintained Dulcinea del Toboso to be the most
beautiful princess in the universe. As this tragedy was
written by a Scotch clergyman; and as it was the first
play he ever had made public, one would have expected,
that he and his friend would have ushered it into the world,
either with a real or affected modesty : but, on the contrary, they declared the play to be perfect, and the author to
be endowed with a genius superior to that of Shakespear and
Otway. The comparison which this extravagant encomium
obliged people to make, has opened the eyes of many who
were at first prevailed upon to be partial to the play ; and
induced them to join the impartial men of sense in both king-
doms, who all agree in thinking it a very insipid performance : so that the author of this tragedy does not a little re-
semble the frog in the fable, who, ambitious to become big
as an ox, blew and puffed himself up till he burst.

The author of the few following pages can't agree with
some, who think the little time spent on such compositions as
this

this very ill bestowed. He can't help numbering the tragedy of DOUGLAS, and the circumstances attending it, amongst the most remarkable occurrences that have ever happened in this country. If Scotch clergymen may, with impunity, not only write plays, but go to see them acted here, and absent themselves for months together from their parishes, in order to solicit their representation at London, the religion and manners of this country are entirely changed. If Shakespear and Otway are to be cried down, and the author of DOUGLAS set up in their stead, the taste of this country is at an end. Religion will (it is hoped) be the care of those who are paid to support it. But the taste of the country seems to be in a deplorable situation, being abandoned to a club of gentlemen, who are as unable as they are willing to direct it. As some men of learning and character are amongst them, many people are misled by their authority; and more, though they detest their innovations, yet are afraid to contradict them: hence it was that DOUGLAS was acted here last winter thirteen times to a numerous audience; but Othello (which had not been played here for seven years) brought no house at all. This shews, that the run DOUGLAS had here, was owing to the influence of a party; or else, that the people who generally compose the audience in our theatre, are no more judges of the merit of a play, than the chairmen who carry them to see it. It is certainly the duty of every man who regards the honour of his country, to make a stand against that unhappy barbarism which the cabal I have already mentioned is endeavouring to establish; and as certainly every man who has felt exquisite pleasure in reading the works of Shakespear and Otway, makes them but a very ungrateful return, if he tamely looks on while they are hunted down by a set of men who owe their title of geniuses to the courtesy of Scotland alone.

THE

# THE
# PHILOSOPHER's
# OPERA.

---

# ACT I.

*A drawing-room.*

*Curtain draws, and discovers Mrs* Sarah Presbytery *sitting in an easy chair;* Anne *waiting.*

*Mrs Pr.* AND did Mr *Genius* talk to you in that manner, *Annie?*

*An.* Indeed the gentleman told me, Madam, that he was desperately in love with you; that he would be miserable, nay, that he would die, if you refused to put him in possession of your fair person; and that he was to throw himself at your feet this afternoon.

*Mrs Pr.* Fie upon the joker; he has been diverting himself, and playing upon you, *Annie.*

*An.* O, not at all, Madam; what should make you think so?

*Mrs Pr.* Alas! *Annie,* I am not young now.

*An.* Young! Madam, what then? he is not young himself. Young! why, there was Lady *Randolph;* I'm

A                                                        sure

sure she was not young; and yet you see how the men teased her, poor lady!

*Mrs Pr.* Alas, *Annie*, I am now about 200 years of age; but Lady *Randolph* broke her neck before she had lived half a century. Go, thou flatterer, thou knowest he has captivated my heart; this, this only, makes you speak so, and give the name of love to what you know to be waggery.

*An.* In my conscience, Madam, I believe him to be over head and ears in love with you. Consider, Madam, that kissing goes by favour. Besides, Mr *Genius*, in his thoughts, words, and actions, has no resemblance to other men; so that you might be his flame, Madam, though you were as old as *Methusalem.*

*Mrs Pr.* There is something in what you say, *Annie.* O the lovely *Adonis*, his shoulders, his legs, his belly! —— But why should I attempt to enumerate his charms? every limb of him is bristled with the darts of love; and would to God I had never seen the too amiable porcupine.

AIR I. Can love be controul'd by advice?
*The goddess who sable Night rules,*
*From* Phœbus *purloins all her light;*
*So I make opticians my tools,*
*And borrow from glasses my sight.*
*Great* Genius, *for whose love this sigh,*    *[sighs.]*
*Was surely created for me,*
*His limbs are so bulky that I*
*Their beauties sans spectacles see.*

*An.* Madam, there is the gentleman.
### Enter Mr Genius.
*Mr Gen.* If Mrs *Anne*, Madam, has delivered that
message

meſſage which I begged her to carry from me to your
Ladyſhip, you will not be ſurpriſed, I hope, at this
piece of intruſion.

*Mrs Pr.* Sir, *Annie* has been telling me of a very
odd converſation ſhe had with you this forenoon; but I
would have you to know, Sir, that I will not be made
a jeſt of by you or any man.

*Mr Gen.* How you miſtake my intentions! there is
not a man in the world more ſenſible of the great deference and reſpect due to you, Madam, than I am.
Jeſt!—— be aſſured, Madam, [*kneeling*], that you ſee
at your feet a man who is determined to live or die as
you receive him.

*Mrs Pr.* Riſe, Mr *Genius*; if you are ſerious, I am
ſorry for you; but I flatter myſelf, you will ſoon perceive the oddity of your paſſion, and the abſurdity of
your choice. The cheek of the town-lady may vie
with the lily, that of the milkmaid with the roſe; but
mine, Sir, can be compared to neither. To uſe my
ſon *Jacky's* words :——" In me thou doſt behold ——
" The poor remains of beauty once admir'd." Age has
deadened the glance of my eye, overcaſt my features with
a melancholy languor, and ploughed my forehead into
a multiplicity of wrinkles.

*Mr Gen.* Pardon me, Madam; age has given to your
eye a philoſophical ſedateneſs, to your features a lan-
guiſhing air, which girls in vain affect; and in what
you call wrinkles, Madam, I ſee the little loves and graces ſporting.

*Mrs Pr.* O Mr *Genius!*

*Mr Gen.* Many gentlemen have wiſhed, Madam, for old
wood to burn, old wine to drink, old friends to converſe

with,

with, and old books to read; but never did I so limit my desires: I have always hoped, that sooner or later I should have an old woman to caress.

*Mrs Pr.* Incomparable *Genius!* I will not use you with the coquetry of a young hussy; but frankly own that I long have loved you.

*Mr Gen.* Is it possible? Words are inadequate to my ideas; and this is the only way my lips can express the sentiments of my heart.

[*He endeavours to kiss her; she struggles, but he prevails.*]

*Mrs Pr.* Lord! Sir, you are such another gentleman.

*Mr Gen.* These breasts, [*putting his hand in her bosom.*]

*Mrs Pr.* Keep off your hands, naughty gentleman that you are.——Nay now, Mr *Genius*, you grow intolerably rude; I shall be seriously angry with you;—— you must wait for the grace, Sir.

*Mr Gen.* Madam, I beg ten thousand pardons, if the violence of my passion has transported me beyond the bounds of decency.—— Yes, Madam, I will wait, and as long as you please; for I am confident, you have more goodness than to make me repent my complaisance.

AIR II. Woe's my heart that we should sunder.

*If you amuse me with vain hope,*
*Till Time's unpitying fingers press us,*
*These my own hands shall knit me up,*
*And put in practice my own essays.*

Mrs Pr. *Imagine not I'll use you so:*
*Perhaps my life is everlasting;*
*But, lovely Genius, well I know,*
*To the church-yard you fast are hasting.*

Let not our interview, Mr *Genius*, end like that of
two

two youthful lovers, without one word of common fenſe
being ſpoken by either of us : Do you go to ſee my
ſon's play to-night ?

*Mr Gen.* I hope for the pleaſure of ſeeing you there,
Madam. What makes you aſk the queſtion ?

*Mrs Pr.* Why, truly, that I may have an opportunity of expreſſing my gratitude. Many of my ſons have
been greatly obliged to you ; but *Jacky* infinitely.

*Mr Gen.* O dear Madam !

*Mrs Pr.* Mr *John Calvin*, my firſt huſband, was a
very good man ; but he had his oddities ; and notwith-
ſtanding the affection which a woman muſt retain for the
huſband of her youth, I cannot help thinking you the
better reformer of the two. Many of my ſons, ſome time
ago, before they had the honour of your acquaintance,
were the moſt unlicked cubs ever were whelped : how
ſtiff was their ſtyle ! how ſtarch their manner ! how ridi-
culouſly grave the whole man ! But ſince they got into
your good company, they have put off the old man entirely : they have acquired a jaunty air, a military ſwag-
ger, and a G—d-d—n-me look ; they ſwear, they drink,
they whore ſo handſomely ; ——in ſhort, they are
metamorphoſed ſo very much to the better, that I
ſcarce know them to be my own children

*Mr Gen.* Your goodneſs, Madam, greatly magnifies
my poor ſervices.

*Mrs Pr.* How judicious was that fancy of yours to
make *Jacky* write a play ! and how inimitable the dedication with which you introduced it into the world ! To
it *Jacky* owes both his fame and his fortune, and ought
to thank you on his knees for both.

*Mr Gen.* The young gentleman, Madam, is abun-
dantly

dantly grateful; but I beg you would dwell no longer
on this subject. I wish it were in my power to do more
for him. I must now leave you, Madam, and join several of your sons who are to be at the playhouse to-
night.

*Mrs Pr.* And I must away to Lady *Prelacy*, who
goes along with me to the same place. Farewell till six
o'clock.                                                    *[Exit.*

*Mr Gen.*    AIR III.    A free and an accepted Mason.
            *Unhappy are you*
            *If a girl you woo;*
    *With rivals you always are fighting:*
            *But I am secure,*
            *And morally sure,*
    *Old women alone I delight in.*

            *Or if you shou'd wed*
            *A blooming young maid,*
    *You, as at a cuckold, all stare on.*
            *The lewdest dragoons*
            *Wou'd see blood and wounds,*
    *Ere my marriage-bed they wou'd share in.*

            *And if ye shall shew*
            *Ye think my love new,*
    *I'll do something still more worth seeing:*
            *For novelty's praise,*
            *To make people gaze,*
    *Is the principal end of my being.*

            *The bride I now leave,*
            *Has one foot in the grave;*
    *My next shall be yet more uncommon:*

                                                    *The*

[ 7 ]

*The church-yard I'll seek,*
*The coffins I'll break,*
*Till I hug some dead buried old woman.*     [*Exit.*


*Arthur's Seat.*


*Enter* Sulphureo.


What can *Apollyo* mean? he promised to meet me here precisely at three o'clock, and now it is hard upon four. Perhaps he is wandering over this mountain in quest of me. Ho, *Apollyo!* ho! hoa! No *Apollyo* here it seems. What does he keep me waiting for? He is not *Garrick* the player, nor am I a young *Scotch* clergyman come a-beseeching him to act my tragedy; he is not a great man, nor am I an old reverend come a-begging some plurality or other, as a reward for my jobs past, present, and to come. No! we are two devils: and having said so much, I need not add, that we are honester fellows than most clergymen.

AIR IV.   'Twas when the seas were roaring.

*They constantly are roaring,*
    *From pulpits hung with green,*
*'Gainst swearing, drinking, whoring,*
    *And ev'ry other sin.*
*Think not, ye simple bearers,*
    *When thus to you they preach,*
*That parsons are practisers*
    *Of what their sermons teach.*

                                       *Their*

*Their habit now is gaudy;*
*Like officers they swear;*
*Their conversation's bawdy:*
*To stage-plays they repair.*
*But if we by this nation*
*Were paid for living well,*
*We wou'd have the discretion*
*Our vices to conceal.*

*Enter* Apollyo *at the other end of the stage.*

*Ap.* Ho, *Sulphureo!* ho! hoa!

*Sulph.* Here, here.

*Ap.* O, your servant, Mr *Sulphureo.*

*Sulph.* I am indeed your servant, Mr *Apollyo;* for I have waited here about an hour for your Honour.

*Ap.* Why, Sir, such a croud of people from this country came upon us this morning, that *Satan* could not get away from hell till a few minutes ago. So that, good Mr *Sulphureo,* I hope you'll excuse us.

*Sulph.* O yes, I do. But will you, *Apollyo,* who are one of our secretaries of state, be so good as to inform me why *Satan* is of late turned so negligent of his affairs in this country. I have been his *aid-de-camp* now for some time, yet I never was in this town before: there is a great change in his behaviour to this country; for I am told, about fifty years ago he used to be very often in *Scotland.*

*Ap.* There he comes, ask himself.

*Enter* Satan.

*Sat.* Well, my lads, how goes it? Have you, *Sulphureo,* ordered matters so that every thing be in readiness for my reception?

*Sulph.* I have, Sir. I saw the Reverend gentleman,

and

and told him that you was to be in *Edinburgh* this afternoon, and would be glad of his company; he said he
would meet you at five o'clock in Mrs *Kitchen*'s.

*Sat*. At five, very well. And how do you like the
good town of *Edinburgh*, *Sulphureo*?

*Sulph*. Good! call you it?

AIR V.   On ev'ry hill, in ev'ry grove.

*In ev'ry street, in ev'ry lane,*
    *In ev'ry narrow slippery close,*
*Nothing but filth is to be seen:*
    *In all of them I stopt my nose.*
        *And ev'ry thing about it shows,*
        *It is a spacious little house.*

*'Tis not the clouds of smoke alone*
    *Which mount, when cookmaids dinner dress;*
*But 'tis the manners of the town,*
    *Which must oblige you to confess,*
        *(Forgiving your* Sulphureo's *mirth),*
        *Auld Reeky is a hell on earth.*

Before you came up to us, I was inquiring at *Apollyo*
how you came to be so indifferent about this country;
you'll pardon my presumption, in begging to know the
reason of this coldness, which to me at present seems to
be mal-administration.

*Sat*. In the days of yore, *Sulphureo*, I was almost
constantly in *Scotland*, and obliged to exert all my met-
tle. Yet, for all that, I own the opposition here fairly got
the better of me, and for a considerable time I had only
a small select society that stuck by me. The ministers
made conscience (as the phrase was in those days) of
doing their duty; the greatest folks lived soberly; and
indeed all ranks of people were in the most deplorable si-

B                                     tuation

tuation you can well imagine. I had very near have given
them up altogether : however, I very luckily had the refo-
lution to perfevere ; a good many years ago the tables
were turned, and now almoft the whole nation is my moft
obedient humble fervant. I am the more delighted with
this conqueft, becaufe, of all the countries I have fub-
dued, this made the moft obftinate refiftance : but now
the moft of its inhabitants are more ingenious in my way
than I myfelf can pretend to be.

AIR VI.    Nanfey's to the green wood gane.

*So when fome wild deceiving boy*
    *Affaults th' unfpotted virgin,*
*At firft the lafs is very coy,*
    *And long refifts his urging.*
*But after fhe is fairly won,*
    *And the foul deed is over,*
*The wanton gypfy, not half done,*
    *Out-paramours her lover.*

Now, *Sulphureo,* I hope I have fatisfied you.

*Sulph.* Perfectly, Sir.    I fee your prefence here is not
at all neceffary.

*Sat.* No, it is not : and it was ceremony, not bufinefs,
that brought me here juft now ; for I have all the reafon
in the world to believe that my people will be too many
for their antagonifts without my affiftance : but as this
is the third night of the firft play ever was written by a
*Scotch* clergyman, I thought the leaft I could do was to
give my countenance to fuch a bold attempt to ferve me.

AIR VII.    Sufannah.

*Good manners would not let me frown*
    *On the young tragic prieft :*

My

*My company and half a crown*
*Was all he did request.*

Sulph. Ap. *The youthful parson to refuse,*
*Sure you had not done well;*
*And to procure him a full house*
*You shou'd have empty'd hell.*

*Sat.* There are to be nine clergymen in the playhouse
to-night. Curiosity to see people of their character in
such a place, would of itself secure the poet of a good
third night; but my emissaries have taken care that he
shall have a full house every night his play is acted.

*Sulph.* I am glad to hear it. Shall I show you the
way to Mrs *Kitchen's*?

*Sat.* Why, we must change our appearance in the
first place. I think I will assume the dress of a country-
gentleman just come from a journey; do you transfigure
yourselves into my footmen. But stay, it is but a few
minutes after four, we shall be too soon if we set out
immediately for Mrs *Kitchen's*; let us climb to the top
of *Arthur's Seat*, the view from it is charming.

AIR VIII. Over the hills and far away.

*Yon mountain's summit when I tread,*
*The prospect will transport my sight;*
*Unlike to* Moses, *who survey'd*
*The holy land from* Pisgah's *height.*

*Pensive he saw the fruitful plains,*
*Plains which he never was to share:*
*All you shall see to me pertains,*
*The possessors my vassals are.*

*End of the* FIRST ACT.

B 2                                          A C T

# ACT II.

*A tavern.*

*Enter* Maſk.

WHO's there? Bring ſome bottles of claret, and a bowl of punch immediately.

*Enter* Satan, Sulphureo, *and* Apollyo.

*Sat.* My dear Mr *Maſk*, I rejoice to ſee you. How does Mrs *Maſk* do, and all your good family?

*Mr Maſk.* Pretty well, Sir, at your ſervice.

*And pray, Sir, when you came from hell,*
*Our friends there did you leave them well?*

*Sat. All well.* Pray ſit down, Mr *Maſk.* How my heart warms to my good old friend! Fill your glaſs, Mr *Maſk.* Let us drink all our abſent friends. [*They drink*]. Have you had any new books lately, Mr *Maſk?*

*Mr Maſk.* O, great variety, Sir.

*Sat.* I aſk for them firſt; becauſe I remember the committee of ways and means, which I had once eſtabliſhed in this country, told me, that new books were commonly my very good friends.

*Mr Maſk.* Commonly they are ſo. We have only one author of note; but his brain is a very good breeder.

*Sat.* What is the gentleman's name?

*Mr Maſk. Mr Genius* is his name. He is the beſt writer againſt Chriſtianity in *Britain*; nay, he gives very broad hints againſt the being of a God.

*Sat.* Come, drink his health.          [*They drink.*]

AIR

AIR IX.  Dear Colin, prevent my warm blushes.

*The miser feels exquisite pleasure*
*In touching a precious bank-note;*
*But I wou'd not give for his treasure,*
*A leaf which an Atheist wrote.*

*When that's chang'd, he no doubt may bring home*
*Some thousands to hide in his holes;*
*But this will convey to my kingdom,*
*Ten thousand times ten thousand souls.*

But hark ye, Mr *Mask*, does he deny my existence?

*Mr Mask.* O! laughs at it, Sir.

*Sat.* How very much surprised will he be when he goes to hell! However, I'll have his works reprinted there *typis regiis*; they well deserve it.

*Mr Mask.* He maintains there is no difference 'twixt right and wrong but what custom has introduced.

*Sat.* How much am I obliged to the gentleman! Dear Sirs, drink his health again. [*They drink.*]. *Encore,* if you please.  Huzza!          [*They drink and huzza!*

*Mr Mask.* He has broached a great number of such propositions.

*Sat.* I should be very glad to see him.

*Mr Mask.* You shall see him very soon.          [*Rings.*

*Enter* Moll Kitchen.

You know where Mr *Genius* is; tell him I must speak with him here.          [*Exit* Moll.

Before this philosopher arrives, I will show you another who has a great many disciples. I know he is over a bottle just now in this house.          [*Rings.*

*Enter* Moll.

Desire Mr *Moral Sense* to step in here for a few minutes,

nutes, and do you follow him. [*Exit.*] This fellow
pretends to be the most generous difinterefted man a-
live; though, in reality, there is not a more felfifh dog
on the face of the earth.

*Enter* Moral Senfe *and* Moll.

*Mor. Senfe.* O my dear gentlemen, how I love all
and every one of you! I would willingly, moft willingly,
lay down my life, fhed my heart's blood, to ferve you,
my dear, dear, dear Gentlemen.

*Sat.* Sir, we are very much obliged to you for your
kindnefs. Will you drink a glafs of wine, Sir?

*Mor. Senfe.* O, with all my heart. I approve of
good wine. Gentlemen, your healths. [*Drinks.*] This
wine is very good. I have an unbounded benevolence
for it. Another glafs, if you pleafe, Sir. [*Drinks.*] O,
Gentlemen, if you knew how much I love you, and your
wine, you would not refufe me a third. [*Drinks.*] Yet
another, Sir, to drink health and happinefs to all mankind. [*Drinks.*] One more.

*Mafk.* Sir, if you will have patience for a few minutes,
you fhall have your bellyfull; but I beg you would
drink no more, till you have given your opinion upon a
point of fome confequence. What do you think of a
marriage 'twixt me and *Moll* there?

*Mor. Senfe.* Hui! Hui! Hui! [*fhrieks hideoufly,*]
it fhocks me; I difapprove of it. But I will lie with
her myfelf. [*Coming up to her.*] I will lie with you,
Moll, [*laying hold of her.*]

*Sat.* Hold! hold, Sir.

*Mor. Senfe.* I will lie with her; I approve of her.
The το καλον fhines in her face. I will lie with you,
Moll. [*Endeavours to throw her,* Satan *interpofes.*]

What

What do you mean, Sir? My instinct prompts me to lie with her.

*Sat.* You impertinent scoundrel, I'll teach your instinct better manners. [*Kicks him off.*] This is a very odd philosopher, Mr *Mask.*

*Mask.* Very odd, indeed, Sir. It is a rule of his, never to think a moment about what he either says or does.——There comes Mr *Genius.*

### Enter Mr Genius.

Mr *Genius,* your servant: This, Sir, is Mr *Bevil,* a friend of mine, [*They salute*], who having red your books with great delight, was very curious to see you face to face.

*Mr Gen.* You have red my books then, Sir?

*Sat.* Yes, Sir, with great delight.

*Mr Gen.* Why, then, Sir, you are convinced, I suppose, that there is no God, no devil, no future state;——that there is no connection betwixt cause and effect;——that suicide is a duty we owe to ourselves;——adultery a duty we owe to our neighbour;——that the tragedy of DOUGLAS is the best play ever was written; and that *Shakespear* and *Otway* were a couple of dunces.——This, I think, is the sum and substance of my writings.

*Sat.* It is, Sir.

AIR X. Leaderhaughs and Yarrow,
*Great* Hercules, Jove's darling son,
*Was forc'd alone to wander;*
*And monsters with his club knock down,*
*To glut his stepdame's anger.*

Shakespear

Shakefpear *and* Otway, *with your pen,*
  *Unforc'd you have run thoro' ;*
*And therefore fhould be held by men,*
  *To be the greater hero.*

*Mr Gen.* O, Sir, you do me too much honour. I'm
forry, Gentlemen, to leave you fo foon; but I am engaged to go to the play with a party of clergymen. [*Exit.*

*Sat.* Mr *Mafk,* I proteft the play had gone out of
my head. You'll accompany us to the playhoufe, I
fuppofe ?

*Mafk.* Not I, indeed.

*Sat.* Why ?

*Mafk.* Why, becaufe your enemies will lay hold of
the proceedings that are to be this night in the playhoufe, and endeavour to ftir up a rebellion againft you.
They will foon prepare overtures and libels againft the
author of this play, and every other minifter who faw it
reprefented. This determines me not to go. I will feem
to be rather againft the author of this play, and his fol-
lowers; by thefe means, I fhall gain the good graces
of the oppofite party, which will enable me to quafh
any violent meafures againft him.

AIR XI. O Beffy Bell and Mary Gray.

*The zealous fools will, if they can,*
  *With depofition end him ;*
*But all our party to a man,*
  *Will vote, Rebuke, fufpend him.*
*Such cenfures will not, I believe,*
  *His tragic genius fmother ;*
*Sufpenfion for one play will give*
  *Him time to write another.*

Sut.

*Sat.* Thou reasonest well.

*Mask.* 'Tis our only way, Sir; but, *Satan*, what do you think of Mr *Genius* ?

*Sat.* 'Faith, I don't know well what to think of him. Are you sure he is true blue on our side? I confess, I have some suspicion, that he is a shrewd fellow, endeavouring to convert men to Christianity, by writing nonsense against it.

*Mask.* You are quite mistaken, Sir: he is reckoned the ablest writer we have; so able, Sir, that all the good folks say, when he wrote his books, he had you at his elbow.

*Sat.* Really, Mr *Mask*, I think I may say without vanity, that had I assisted him, he would not have written so absurdly. I was very well pleased to hear him deny the existence of a God, and so forth; but his positions about suicide and adultery will certainly do our cause no good.

AIR XII. Hooly and fairly.

*With bearing his nonsense in troth I am weary ;*
*That nonsense will hurt me much, I can assure ye ;*
*And make many people believe most sincerely.*
*O! gin the lad wad write hooly and fairly,*

*Hooly and fairly, &c.*
[*Exeunt.*

**End of the SECOND ACT.**

A C T

# ACT III.

*A drawing-room.*

*Enter Mrs* Presbytery, *Miss* Weepwell, *Miss* Pity, *Miss* Sob, *Miss* Blubber.

*Mrs Pr.* LADIES, now that you have seen my son *Jacky's* play, let me have your opinions on it impartially.

*Miss Weep.* I believe, Madam, this company will be very unanimous in voting it to be the best play ever was written.

*Mrs Pr.* O, don't flatter me, Ladies.

*Miss Blub.* The tears, Madam, you saw shed in the playhouse, may convince you, that, without flattery, we are all of Miss *Weepwell's* opinion.

*Enter Miss* Sprightly.

*Miss Spr.* Your servant, Ladies.

*Mrs Pr.* My dear Miss *Sprightly!*

*Miss Weep.* Bless me, child, your eyes are not at all red.

*Miss Spr.* What should make them so?

*Miss Weep.* Weeping.

*Miss Spr.* For what?

*Miss Weep.* Was not you at the play?

*Miss Spr.* Yes, I was.

*Miss Weep.* Have you not then been crying for these three hours?

*Miss Spr.* Not I.

*Miss Weep.* Cruel creature!

*Miss*

*Miſs Spr.* Why cruel, pray?

*Miſs Weep.* Not to weep for DOUGLAS.

*Miſs Spr.* What ſhould make me weep for him?

*Miſs Weep.* Not to weep for ſuch a hero!

*Miſs Spr.* What makes you dub him a hero, in all the world?

*Miſs Weep.* Did not he kill the chief robber?

*Miſs Spr.* And does that make him a hero?

### AIR XIII.

*Had DOUGLAS liv'd on Engliſh ground,*
*Where highwaymen, you know, abound;*
*And there, by the good-will of Fate,*
*Some noted robber's brains out beat;*
    *A warrior's fame,*
    *Or hero's name,*
*He in that country ne'er had found.*
    *The ſturdy lad*
    *Wou'd juſt have had*
*A premium of neat forty pound.*

*Miſs Weep.* You may carp as much as you will, Miſs, at ſome particular places of the play; but you will own, no doubt, that, upon the whole, it is the beſt play ever was written.

*Miſs Spr.* Will I ſo?

*Miſs Weep.* Pray, who has written a better?

*Miſs Spr. Shakeſpear, Otway* ———

*Miſs Weep.* Hold! the very naming of theſe two fellows is enough to make one ſick. Sure, child, you have not red Mr *Genius's* dedication.

*Miſs*

*Miſs Spr.* AIR XIV. *Clout the caldron.*
*In lapdogs, laces, hoops, ſtays, fans,*
  *And all your other tackle,*
*Howe'er capricious you may be,*
  *I care not, or how fickle:*
*But yet, for all great Genius ſays,*
  *I really can't help wiſhing,*
*That* Shakeſpear, Otway, *and their plays,*
  *May ne'er go out of faſhion.*

*Fa adrie didle didle, &c.*

*Miſs Weep.* Miſs *Sprightly,* I am not a little ſurpriſed to hear you talk at this rate. Sure neither you nor I can pretend to be ſuch good judges as Mr *Jacky* and Mr *Genius;* and you know very well, what contempt they have for *Shakeſpear* and *Otway.*

*Miſs Spr. Jacky* and *Genius,* very pretty fellows truly!

AIR XV. Gill Morris.

*By the remains of* Scottiſh *youth,*
  *Who taſte untainted boaſt,*
*Let all the paltry works of both*
  *To raging flames be toſt.*
*This holocauſt alone can ſooth*
  *Great* Shakeſpear's *injur'd ghoſt.*

*Enter Mr* Genius.

*Miſs Weep.* You are come in good time, Sir. We have had a ſtout battle with Miſs *Sprightly* about the tragedy of DOUGLAS. She has been running it down very warmly.

*Mr Gen.* I am ſorry to hear it: for ſtill her lips muſt be rubies, and her voice melody, though both be employed againſt the beſt play ever was written.

Mrs

[ 21 ]

*Mrs Pr.* [*aside.*] So, so: this young *Jackanapes* will not only rob the son of his glory, but the mother of her gallant.

*Enter Mr Jacky.*

*Miss Weep.* O, Mr *Jacky*, your servant. I give you joy, Sir. [*They all advance, and salute him.*] I give you joy, Sir, that your tragedy has met with that success which the best play ever was written deserves. You, Sir, possess the true theatric genius of *Shakespear* ——

*Miss Sob.* And *Otway* ——

*Miss Pity.* Refined from the unhappy barbarism of the one ——

*Miss Blub.* And licentiousness of the other.

*Jacky.* O Ladies! nay, dear Ladies!

*Mrs Pr.*   Air XVI. Black Jock.

*Dear Sir, and dear Ladies, my* Jacky *is young,*
*And bashfulness hinders the thanks of his tongue,*
   *For filling his pockets with half-crowns so white.*
*He's sensible 'twas not the musical lasses,*
*Who dance, sing, and play on the top of* Parnassus,
   *But you who got him the half-crowns so white.*

*To thee, noble* Genius, *the knee he shou'd bow;*
*More than to* Apollo *to thee does he owe:*
      Shakespear *scoffing,*
      Douglas *puffing,*
*You screw'd mens opinions to such a great height,*
*That they filled his pockets with half-crowns so white.*

*Jacky.* Dear mother, you have very handsomely expressed my gratitude, which a foolish bashfulness would not allow me to do. In return, I must insist on your giving to Mr *Genius* your hand; which a bashfulness, still more foolish than mine, will not, I hope, make you refuse.

refuse. I know you love one another; your marriage to-night will consummate my happiness.

*Mrs Pr.* There, Sir, is my hand; you long have had my heart.

*Mr Gen.* Madam, I am so very sensible of the honour you do me, that I here vow and swear never more to write essays, discourses, histories, dissertations; but to make your entertainment the sole study of my life.

AIR XVII. Logan water.

*Two hundred years tho' you be old,*
*And tho' your youthful bloom be fled,*
*Yet fear not, dearest, I'll prove cold,*
*Or loiter when we are in bed.*

Mrs Pr. *Two hundred years tho' I be old,*
*And tho' my youthful bloom be fled,*
*Yet fear not, dearest, I'll prove cold;*
*I'll be but twenty when in bed.*

*Miss Weep.* This is the only farce I could have endured to see after the tragedy of DOUGLAS. Let us have fiddles, and a dance.

[*They dance. Satan, Sulphureo, and Apollyo enter in their true shape, and offer to dance along with them; but they all run off.*

*Sat.* Ay, why in such a hurry? The devil will not give himself the trouble to take the hindmost, I assure ye; for he is pretty certain to meet with all of you time and place more convenient. Well, my lads, how did you like DOUGLAS?

*Sulph.* It is a very moving tragedy, Sir; the tears are in my eyes yet. [*Wiping his eyes.*

*Ap.* And in mine too.

EXit.

*Sat.* I agree with Mr *Genius*, in thinking it the best play ever was written. I could descant upon it all night; but we had better keep our observations for *Mask*, who will by this time be longing much for us, and more for his supper. Let us to Mrs *Kitchen's*, and be merry.

AIR XVIII.   Jolly mortals, fill your glasses.

> *Jolly devils, drink I charge ye,*
> *Pass in sport the time away;*
> *Bumpers swill to all the clergy,*
> *Who or write or see a play.*
>
> *Now I wou'd not give three guilders,*
> *For the superstitious fry;*
> *You shall all be ruling elders,*
> *And the moderator I.*

*F I N I S,*

# Gretna Green

*26d*

# GRETNA GREEN,

## A

## COMIC OPERA,

### IN TWO ACTS

AS PERFORMED AT THE

*THEATRE ROYAL, SMOKE-ALLEY.*

---

PRINTED FOR THE BOOKSELLERS.

## DRAMATIS PERSONÆ.

Rory, the Black-smith and Parson.
Captain Tipperary.
Captain Gorget.
Andrew, and a Farrier.
Post-Boy.
Postillion.

Miss Plump.
Maria.
Signiora.
Lady Pedigree.

# GRETNA GREEN.

## ACT I.—SCENE I.

*An outside View of a Blacksmith's Shop a distant View of Mountains, &c. RORY discovered with two Assistant Farriers.*

AIR I. *by* RORY, *who comes from the Shop.*

I Can shoe a horse or kiss a lass
   And nail twa lovers firm as brass,
I can knock about the pot and glass
   In bumpers till I'am mellow:
Ye parents guardians I defy,
Nay e'ven the Court of Chancery,
The widow's tears the virgin's sigh
   I stop like a good fellow.
Old maidens I detest,
Peevish fretting, yet coquetting,
Batchelors can ne'er be blest,
   Snarling and backbiting.

All ye fair wards pray come to me,
 I'll grant you Hymen's liberty
To love and sport with merry glee,
   As mammy did before ye:
Then all ye bucks and bloods and beaux,
Bring each your girls that are not foes,
To wedding shoes, and wedding cloaths
   As daddy did before ye.
Old maidens, &c.

### Enter ANDREW.

Come master Rory, here's more work for you mon.
   RORY. Huzza! gude news faith, then I may light
Hymen's Torch at the Forge of Vulcan, and Cupid
may blaw the Bellows.

AND.

AND. Ay mafter Rory, you have always two irons i' the fire.

RORY. Twa irons, three if you pleafe, firft of aw J'm a Blackfmith, fecondly I'm a Doctor of Phyfic (for horfes,) thirdly I'm a Doctor for Lovers, for many a couple has their hands coupl'd in wedlock.— Well madam mafter Crack (Enter POSTILION.) have you brought me any more cuftomers.

POST. Yes, an Irifh officer, with a young lady from London, and an Italian Madamazell with them, they are a rare fprightly fet—the Irifhman lather'd away as he call'd it, and odsflefh, at every kifs he gave his bride, he made a fmack as loud as my whip (fnaps his whip) but here they come.

*Enter* TIPPERARY *and* Mifs PLUMB.

(as he enters) Where the devil has the boy got?

POST. There he calls me boy that has a wife and fix children.

TIP. Which is the parfon-my dear?

POST. There he is.

TIP. What that blackguard there! Is that the parfon. Pray friend now tell me are you a Proteftant Clergyman or a Prefbyterian, or are—perhaps you are a White Friar.

RORY. In troth captain I am a Black Friar at your fervice.

TIP. Can you marry a gentleman, and will your marriages ftand good in law?

RORY. Aye, in any Court of Chriftendom, even in Chancery.

Mifs PLUMB. Oh yes, captain, for I have heard fay any body may marry in Scotland.

RORY. (looks attentively at Tipperary) it certainly muft be the fame—it is the very man of aw, (afide.) a word with you captain, did I not once marry you before?

TIP. Why what the devil friend!—was it you did me that kind office? but hufh! my honeft Parfon— I'll be your cuftomer again fhortly,

RORY. Oh, I am mum.

Mifs PLUMB. What is any thing the matter captain?

TIP.

TIP. Oh nothing my jewel at all ; only the parson here says, he longs to be marrying so handsome a couple my dear.

RORY. Aye that I do—here Andrew *(Enter AN-DREW.)* get me my Canoneals, in the intrum I'll give you a song I learn't from a countryman of yours, he was an unco good customer of mine—I married him three times in a twelve-month.

From fair London City we set out post flying,
   And the two horns at Highgate we past in a crack ?
Cheek by jowl life and soul day and night plying,
   On dashing jades slashing they fly at each smack ;
From fair London, &c.

Whip and spur bur hur rur all the way splashing,
   Driving and prancing and spanking along ;
Laughing and galloping quaffing and walloping
   And squeaking like two little pigs in a throng.
Whip and spur, &c.             [*Exit.*

TIP. By my Soul, that's a queer son of a whore of a parson—Well my jewel tell me how you are after your journey.

MISS PLUMB. Oh! never in better spirits : but my head is so full of matrimony, that I forgot poor Signiora my governess.

TIP. Aye, by my conscience, so did I myself forgot her—poor Signiora—but here she comes.

### Enter SIGNIORA.

SIG. Ay! you be de great run away.

MISS PLUMB. Oh! Signiora I wish I was married, and it was all over ; lord bless me I shall be so ashamed.

SIG. And I shall be ashamed too—Shant you be ashamed captain.

TIP. Aye, that I shall my honey, my cheeks will be redder than my regimentals--after the day of wedding Signiora—I will give you a thousand pounds out of Miss Plumb's fortune,

SIG. Aye, that will comfort poor Signiora : a marriage be one pleasant thing.

A 3                      Soft

Soft Arno's stream how sweet divine
　　As on its fl'w'ry banks we rove,
Its cooling shades and neat Cassino
　　Rural appears the seat of love.
There Tuscan youths in sweet Soprano,
　　Whisper the soothing am'rous tale:
There Tuscan maids in soft Piano
　　Coo, murm'ring with the sighing gale.

O lead me to the calm Reposo
　　Where all the loves and graces dwell,
Where every swain Affettuoso,
　　Tenderly sighs his flame to tell;
Were every maid dissolves in blisses,
　　Cara! oh Cara! waft me there.
Where pains and sorrows die in kisses,
　　Kisses that charm and heal despair.
　　　　　　　　　　[*Exit with* Miss Plumb.

TIP. The devil burn me, but it is not clear to me but I shall marry Signiora too.

*Enter* RORY *with black gown and band, &c.*

RORY. Here I am captain—you see me now black and all black.

TIP. Yes, yes, you look something like a priest now.

*Enter* WOMAN *and* POST BOY.

BOY. Maister Rory, maister Rory, there's the bairne waiting to be christen'd.
　　　　　　　　　　*Exit* Woman *and* Boy.

RORY. Very well I was just agoing.

*Enter* ANDREW.

AND. Sandy's mair is just a-dying, and they want you to see what's the matter with her.

*Enter* POSTILLION.

RORY. Well maister Crack.

POST. The couple are waiting to be married, and I shall lose my job.

RORY. Very well I was just agoing—the mair may die if she will, and the child an Annabaptist, but I must go and marry Captain Tipparary wi aw convenient dispatch.

　　　　　　　　　　　　　　　　TIP.

T<small>IP</small>. Get out ye wagabonds all of you. *(beats them off with his cane——singing heard by* Maria.) Ha! there's a pretty Girl yonder—I fuppofe fhe wants to be married too.

R<small>ORY</small>. Very like, very like the couples come down to Gretna Green wi as muckle willingnefs and as faft as the couples went into the Ark.

T<small>IP</small>. Pray now what is the name of that pretty girl yonder?

R<small>ORY</small>. She lives in this neighbourhood: they call her Jeffie of the Tweed, or the little Shepherdefs, fhe has liv'd here this fortnight; and na one can tell from whence fhe came, or what fhe is doing.

[Maria *fings again within.*

T<small>IP</small>. Upon my honour now fhe fings like any Canary-bird.

R<small>ORY</small>. I perceive captain you are a good Mufician —I fuppofe you play on aw forts of inftruments.

T<small>IP</small>. Aye by foul maifter Clergyman, and I like all inftruments, but one do you fee.

R<small>ORY</small>. What is that, captain?

T<small>IP</small>. The Scotch Fiddle my dear!

R<small>ORY</small>. You are a wag, you are a wag, captain— but you muft allow that the Scotch are a harmonious people for they have mufic at their finger ends.— Now for my ain part give me the mufical glaffes, and a gude bottle before me.

T<small>IP</small>. Oh oh! my dear, fo you make your bottle your miftrefs—well then you are right, for it is a mighty pretty amufement.

R<small>ORY</small>. Very well, very well,—but notwithftanding your jokes, it has its comforts let me tell you.

> My bottle is my wife and friend,
>   When low her fpirits rear me,
> If ever Rory does unbend,
>   Oh how her fpirit chears me.
>     Lovely bottle,
>     Warms my throttle,
> Makes me niddle noddle queerly;
>     Stammer ftumble,
>     Stare and tumble,
> Wimble womble dearly.

She

She is my doctor and my nurfe,
   My champion in a hobble;
Altho' fhe empties oft my purfe,
   She makes my blood right noble.
     Lovely bottle, &c.

When by the waift I feize my wife
   She fires me with love ftories;
As I'm wedded to her firm for life,
   I'll dance and fing her glories.
     Lovely bottle, &c.      [*Exit.*

TIP. The devil burn me but he's a comical fellow.
*(looks after him.)*

*Enter* MARIA *with a book.*

I laugh, I dance, I pipe, I fing,
   And merrily pafs the hours away,
Each morn does fome new blefling bring,
   That keeps me ever blithe and gay:

My food is hope, my drink is joy,
   My wealth is a pure and lively mind,
My happinefs knows no alloy,
   Unlefs when pity fays be kind.

TIP. Upon my honour mifs, you fing divinely, if
it had not been for your petticoat, I fhould take you
for a pretty little bird.

MAR. I perceive fir, you are a judge and one of the
conufcenti.

TIP. Conufcenti, madam!

MAR. Yes fir, you play on a great variety of in-
fruments I imagine, as you feem fo inchanted with
the fcience.

TIP. Inftrument! what inftrument?

MAR. The harpficord or violin.

TIP. The harpfichord or violin do you fay? by
my confcience I believe I cou'd my dear, becaufe why
do you fee, I never tried, but indeed my dear little
fhepherdefs, I fhou'd like to be playing on fuch a
pretty inftrument as you—Pray my fweet girl, what
book is that you read?

                          MAR.

MAR. I was reading Pope's paftorals.

TIP. Pope! oh, I perceive you are a good catholic, but no matter for that.

MAR. I read fir—I digeft.

TIP. You read and then digeft!—what you read after dinner—what religion do you profefs my dear?

MAR. I profefs to be the friend of all mankind, my mind is liberal and poffeffes univerfal charity to all my fellow creatures.

TIP. Come my fhepherdefs you muft give me a kifs —*(fhe avoids him.)* what, don't you love a foldier?

MAR. Indeed I do, with all my heart.

TIP. Why then I'll take one kifs for the honour of the cloth. *(kiffes her.)*

### Enter Mifs PLUMB.

*(Runs up to* Tipperary*)* Very well fir, very well, if I thought it wou'd have come to this, I wou'd not have thrown fnuff in my father's and mother's eyes, to elope with you and jump out of the window into your arms—you falfe hearted man—a pretty return you make to all my kindnefs—and *(to* Maria,*)* you mifs may be afhamed to talk to other people's fweet-hearts.

MAR. Don't be under any apprehenfions on my ac-count—I have an Irifh captain of my own, full of love, honor, truth, and bravery.

My fond heart fweetly bafks in the bright beams of hope,
Without it thefe rofes and lillies would droop:
'Tis the fun that illumes this parterre of true love;
Without hope I fhould droop like the 'lorn turtle dove.
When my Jamie brav'd danger on Gib'ralter's fell rock,
Hope kept off the balls, made my heart ftand the fhock,
And drew him return'd in all vict'ry's grand charms,
After conq'ring his foes to fubmit to thefe arms.

TIP. You muft not be jealous before marriage my jewel—befides you know we fhall be married foon, and then you may have me all to yourfelf—for a fort-night perhaps. *(Afide.)*

### Enter RORY.

Aye captain I fee very well that you are playing
over

over the old game—why man you appear like the afs
between two bundles of hay.

[*Exit* Captain *and* Rory.

SERVANT *enters and gives* MARIA *a letter.*

(*Reads.*) " This is to inform you my fweet Maria,
" that I am fafe arrived from Gibraltar.—I have
" been rob'd of a few inconfiderable articles, but fhall
" make all poffible hafte to Gretna Green, there to
" enjoy the fuperlative happinefs of embracing my
" ever dear Maria."—(*kiffes the letter*) My dear, my
conftant Gorget !

(Maria *walks fretting at the upper end of the
fage——comes down.*)

Mifs PLUMB. Cruel falfe hearted man to ufe me fo.

MAR. Indeed my dear I would recommend it to
you to go home.

Mifs PLUMB. Home mifs ! Pray why fhould I go
home ?——I came here to marry a hufband, and I
will marry a hufband—go home indeed ! perhaps I
have as great occafion for a hufband as you mifs. (*with
a fneer and vexation.*)

MAR. Have you ever my dear view'd the confe-
quences of matrimony properly in your own mind, do
you know the requifites to make a good wife, and live
happily.

Mifs PLUMB. Yes, to be fure I do, as well as other
people, I muft drefs to walk with my hufband in
Kenfington Gardens on a Sunday—to go to the opera
on a Monday, Hay-market, on Tuefday, Aftley's
on Wednefday, the Circus on Thurfday, Sadler's
Wells on Friday, and to dance on Saturday in Pud-
ding Lane, and walk with my hufband as far as
Paper's Country Houfe in Cold-bath Fields.

See Lady Tonifh of Grofv'nor place,
How charmingly fhe enamels her face,
She pencils her veins with azure blue,
With black her eye brows, combs them too,
    She paints fo true
    In nature's hue,
With red and white Olympian dew,
As makes her look like a doll quite new,

                                        And

And shoots macaronies thro' and thro',
    Thro' and thro', &c.

She drives so furious hand in hand,
Tears up the pavement in the Strand.
Along Pall Mall so swift she goes
She scarce has time to nod at beaux.
    Up St. James's Street,
    She gallops so fleet, .
The bucks at Brooke's cannot her greet ;
For ere from play they can move their feet,
She's tipping the Go-bye in next Street, -
    In next Street, &c.

### Enter RORY.

My bonnie lassie, I believe you have lost your husband the captain.

Miss PLUMB. Well if I have I am determin'd to get
another directly.

RORY. I left the false loon talking to a tall widow
lady, who between ourselves looks as if she wanted a
spice of my office too.

MAR. Do you know her name.

Miss PLUMB. I lay a wager, its my mamma, did
she enquire who threw snuff in her eyes.

RORY. Her name let me see ?—they call her
Pedigree.

MAR. Lady Pedigree!—then I'm undone.

### Enter SIGNIORA.

Ah poor Signiora, here be your mamma and I shall
be turn'd away.

RORY. An you are my bonnie lassie I will take you
into keeping myself; you shall be my interpretor—
what a pity it is that they made the act against
polygandy, if that was not the case, instead of couples they would flock to Gretna Green in droves
like horned cattle, but as to that matter—it is not
long after they leave me but they turn to Horn Cattle
themselves.

Miss PLUMB. I wonder where Captain Tipperary is.

RORY. Now here I am, like Vulcan among the
graces.

                                Blind

Blind Cupid darts ftrike ev'ry one
At random as they fly,
From fparkling glafs and jolly can
They fhoot and blind my eye,
CHOR. What brightens nature's darkeft nights
But love that beauteous boy,
The moon is Hymen's torch that lights,
Each loving pair to joy.

MAR. Impatient I for Thyrfis wait,
And at his bleft return,
He'll find his tender conftant mate
With pureft paffion burn,
CHOR. What brightens nature's darkeft nights,
But love that beauteous boy,
The moon is Hymen's torch that lights,
Each loving pair to joy.

Mifs P. Then I to London fhall return,
For tho' not yet Sixteen,
I'll danger for a hufband fpurn,
And drive to Gretna Green.
CHOR. What brightens nature's darkeft nights,
But love that beauteous boy,
The moon is Hymen's torch that lights,
Each loving pair to joy.

SIG. Then I to th' Op'ra will repair,
For that's the charming fpot,
Where Veftris danc'd with heav'nly air,
Seftini thrill'd her note,
CHOR. What brightens nature's darkeft nights,
But love that beauteous boy,
The moon is Hymen's torch that lights,
Each loving pair to joy.

ACT.

## A C T II.

SCENE—*A mean Apartment in a Scot's Inn,*

*Enter* TIPPERARY.

NOW where the devil is this same widow; here landlord.

*Enter a* LANDLORD.

Your honour called.

TIP. I want to know whereabouts the lady is that I saw juſt now.

LAND. What the lady that arrived here this morning—my Lady Pedigree—oh, ſhe is coming this way. [*Exit.*

TIP. Very well friend—ſhe a lady too!—oh, my pretty Miſs Plumb, I'll leave you to hang upon the tree, until you drop off yourſelf, like a wither'd apple, for I'll ſtick to Lady Pedigree, becauſe ſhe has a much greater fortune, and being an old tabby I ſhall the ſooner get rid of her, for the devil take me if I would tie myſelf to any woman for more than three months, and faith that's long enough for any reaſonable ſoul—but here ſhe comes, and a tight bit of goods, only they are old ſhop keepers, that the worſt on't.

*Enter Lady* PEDIGREE.

(*Walks up and down while* Tipperary *views her, then he ſalute her.*)

TIP. Now what the devil ſhall I ſay to her? But no matter ſhe's a widow, and any thing ſoft.—Madam your moſt obedient ſervant—I perceive that you're a lady wandering by yourſelf, which is a contradiction in nature—I ſuppoſe you are a lady that wants a gentleman, now I am a gentleman that wants a lady, and one that can do the thing for you, ſo if you pleaſe we'll get the blackſmith of a parſon to marry us immediately.

Lady PED. Indeed ſir—No, you miſtake me entirely ſir—I did not come here to marry, but to prevent a marriage.—There is an officer who has inveigled

B

veigled away a foolish girl of mine and wants to dishonour my family by a Scotch marriage.

TIP. Does he my dear? Well then I am officer too, and I will honour your family by an Irish marriage.

Lady PED. Were I so disposed I could have no reasonable objection to your person, but your blood sir, I must be satisfied as to your blood, sir.

TIP. Oh! by my soul, my lady, my blood is as pure as a young goats's upon the mountains of Wicklow yonder.

Lady PED. That may be sir, but is your blood as ancient as mine, sir.

TIP. O! no just, you are right there—it is not so ancient as yours, because why, it is not so old as yours, my dear,—But tell me shall we be married? what you are dumb—but silence you know gives consent my honey, I'll take you at your word and smother you with kisses my dear lady. (*offers to kiss her.*)

Lady PED. Hold captain, if I was ever so well inclined to marry, it is necessary at my time of life, to have a little discretion.

TIP. You are right, for by my conscience you are no chicken.

Lady PED. Besides sir, my family—I am lineally descended from the Princess Spota, who stole the crown from her father the king of the Egyptians.

TIP. What the devil so you are descended from both a thief and a gypsey.

Lady PED. How sir?

TIP. Oh, my lady, your whole family were thieves, and your sweet pretty self is the greatest thief of them all.

Lady PED. What, do you mean to affront me?

TIP. No, my lady, your family were remarkable for stealing crowns, but you are remarkable for stealing hearts, my lady.

Lady PED. Oh, sir——(*curtsying.*)

TIP. Pray madam did you see the coach and six bay horses that stood at the door this morning.

Lady PED. No, sir.

TIP. They were mine my lady, I sent it to fetch half a dozen lords of my acquaintance in this neighbourhood

bourhood to honour my wedding with their company.

Lady Ped Indeed, fir.

Tip. Yes, madam, I keep a Swifs porter, a Ruffian footman, a French cook, and a German fecretary, my lady.

Lady Ped. You are, indeed, a very happy man.

Tip. Oh, yes my lady, and for riches, my poffeffions are fo extenfive, the devil be in me if any body knows either their begining or their end.

*Enter* Rory.

Aye, captain I fee what you are about, I fhall puff you with bellows, and blow up your whole fcheme.

Tip. Be eafy, my friend, when I marry this lady I'll give you five Guineas.

Rory, Will you, then I care not how foon you are ready to be wed.

Lady Ped. Stop friend, I came here to hinder a marriage.

Rory. What's that, my lady, then you are no friend to procreation, but an enemy to the king and the conftitution.

Tip. Yes, and the multiplication table into the bargain.

Rory. If that was the cafe I might put out the fire, and fhut up my fhop.

I faw a ftout fellow ride very queer,
  Hotchity, botchity, fhakity, quakity,
Sweat run down his face with fear
  And the mane he held as the bridle.
To keep him faft on he ftuck fpurs in her fide,
  Kickity, ftickity, frifkity, whifkity,
The faddle flip'd round and he ftuck to her fide,
  And d'ye think my good folks he was idle.

He rode not along, but acrofs the highway,
  Stumblety, tumblety, hitchity, ditchity!
O what a good foul! for his prayers he did fay
  When on the ground he lay bawling,
I quickly to his relief bent my courfe,
  Runnity, funnity, gigglety, nigglety.!

B 2                                     How.

How I laugh'd when I faw neither man nor hor.e,
But a mare, and a taylor, a fprawling.

TIP. Now take me to be your hufband my lady,
and if t at fellow of a parfon marries any one without
my confent, I'll break every bone in his body.

Lady PED. Well, fir, I will confider of your pro-
pofals, I muft not be like the young flirts of the age,
who are ready to take any thing for the fake of a
hufband.　　　　　　　　　　　　　　　　[Exit.

*Enter* SIGNIORA FIGURANTE.

(*Difcovering* Lady Pedigree *taking leave.*)

SIG. Ah, ah, Mr. Captain.

TIP. Aye, my pretty Signiora.

SIG. Go, you be very wicked lover.

TIP. I muft kifs you, Signiora, you remember
that I promis'd you a thoufand pounds out of Mifs
Plumb's fortune.

SIG. Ah! poor Signiora; has but one bank note.

TIP. What do you fay? have you got a bank note?
what is the worth?

SIG. I be worth—let a me fee—I be worth two
hundred and eleventy three pounds.

TIP. Two hundred and eleventy three pounds!
now, with all my learning, the devil fetch me if I
know how much that is, damn me, but, however, I
have a great mind to marry Signiora too.

SIG. Do you love me?

TIP. Yes, by my foul do I beft of all.

SIG. Oh! you be roguifh lover; you love this body,
and that body, and t'other body.

TIP. Faith you are right, old or young I attack
hem all.

SIG. Ah! you be very falfe heart indeed.

Away you wild inconftant lover,
　　You'll never win me by your wiles,
All your deceit I now difcover,
　　The faithlefs vow and look beguiles.
Then fince I find that you're a rover,
　　In vain are roguifh arts and fmiles,

　　　　　　　　　　　　　　**Away**

Away you wild inconftant lover,
  You'll never win me by your wiles, &c.
                              [*Exeunt.*

SCENE *changes to another Room.*

*Enter* GORGET *and* MARIA.

GOR. My faithful, dear Maria, your love and con-
ftancy more than reward me for the dangers and
difficulties I have encounter'd fince I beheld you
laft.

MAR. Aye, my dear Gorget, I never forgot to be
alarmed for your fafety.

Since that dear day my heart you gain'd,
  On the wild thyme bank where vi'lets blow,
For you alone this pipe was ftrain'd,
  For you alone this breaft cou'd glow.
How often have I penfive ftray'd,
  To th' tree where you engrav'd my name,
And when I faw each letter fade
  I cry'd you had fall'n a prey to fame.

GOR. My fweet Maria, what do I not owe you.

MAR. When late I watch'd by the light of the
bright Moon round a neighbouring village, (as foli-
tary walks have been too frequent with me) my eyes
were fuddenly fix'd on a poor maim'd foldier lying on
the cold ground and begging a donation; I reliev'd
his neceffities two fold, for he brought into my anxious mind, fears for the fafety of my dear, my conftant Gorget.

GOR. Maria I find you are continually painting
out why I ought to love you more and more, to re-
lieve the diftrefs'd foldier was an act of humanity as
well as duty—we fhould endeavour to render the
evening of their days happy, for who can behold a
brave man who has loft his limbs in the fervice of his
king and country, without dropping the fympathifing
tear of gratitude.

With honour's fcars
Retir'd from wars
          B 3                          The

The Vet'ran he's a noble fight,
     His ftains are all
     By fword and ball
Thofe crimfon badges of his might.
     His tales infpire
     Heroic fire,
In ev'ry youthful breaft around,
     With valour's ftrong fhield,
     For their king they take the field,
And retire in old age full of glory crown'd.

MAR. Don't you fee a gentleman and lady out yonder—they are a couple juft arrived at this fpot for the purpofe that we are, he an Irifhman and his name Tipperary.

GOR. Why fure I fhould know that face—oh no it can't be him I am certain—I wifh I could fee his face—no it is not poffible—befides my fervant was a Scotchman.——

MAR. My deareft love—my mamma is at Gretna Green, and is come on purpofe to hinder our marriage.

GOR. Lady Pedigree here; then I regret I did not fall at Gibraltar, defending that fortrefs under the noble Veteran that commanded it.

September the thirteenth proud Bourbon may mourn.
     Elliot's light'nings and thunders,
     Like Jove's bolts did wonders,
With fhot, red hot, Don Moreno was torn.
On the hills the fpectators with grief rend the fky.
     There fhips are all on fire
     Hark! what fhricks! fome expire.
     Up they blow, up they blow
     And thoufands now go, to the bottom low,
Whilft wreck'd hundreds defpairing, for fafety loud cry,
And they find it in Curtis's humanity.

           [*Exeunt.*

           SCENE

### SCENE *changes.*

*Enter* RORY, SIGNIORA, *and* Miss PLUMB.

Miss PLUMB. Ah! Signiora—I have loft my captain—however fince he is gone I am refolv'd to die a maid.

RORY. By my troth Mifs and that would be a unco great pity ; but gang with me a while and I'll find you another captain.

Miss PLUMB. Oh! no, I'll never marry another, that I am determin'd—but is your captain as handfome as mine.

RORY. Oh! he is a perfect Adonis—come I'll take you till him : but my bonne laffie never think of dying a maid, for that would be fetting a bad example, and Gretna Green might then go a begging.

*Exeunt* Rory *and* Miss Plumb.

SIG. Every body marry——but nobody marry poor Signiora.

> From branch to branch the feather'd pair
>   Fly chirping on the pleafing ftrain,
> The cares of love : their only care
>   And paffion foothe's their heart felt pain,
> Hark ! liften to the Nightingale,
>   Whofe mellow note falute the fpring :
> On yonder fpray fhe loves to wail.
>   And tenderly tho' fadly fing.

[*Exit.*

### SCENE *changes.*

*Enter* Gorget *and* Maria.

GOR. The arrival of Lady Pedigree is unfortunate beyond meafure.

### *Enter* Lady PEDIGREE.

Lady PED. *(angrily)* Well my pretty runaway, are you not afham'd to bring me fo far after you—but now you may go wander as a fhepherdefs over the heath again, for you have loft my affection I affure you. And you, Sir, *(t* Gorget) you have acted a very honourable part truly : but you may now go and

mourn

mourn over each other like two turtle doves, for to punish you I shall marry Captain Tipperary, and perhaps be bless'd with a child that's dutiful.

MAR. Oh! sir!——

GOR. Don't despair Maria—we will endeavour to be happy notwithstanding.

### *Enter* TIPPERARY.

TIP. Come, my Lady Pedigree, I am waiting with the utmost impatience for the honour of your hand.

GOR (*aside.*) My servant Archy M'Nab who robb'd me.

TIP. My Master!—The devil!—

GOR. Your servant Captain Tipperary—why how the rascal is confounded.—How dare you sir assume the distinguished character of an officer and an Irishman.

TIP. I took the character of an officer to recommend me to the world at large, and I assumed that of an Irishman to recommend me to the ladies at large.

Lady PED. What? is he not an officer? nor an Irishman—what a discovery is this? and what ruin have I escap'd!

GOR. No, madam, his dress he has robb'd me of, and as for the brogue he has borrow'd that from some Irish hay-maker.

### *Enter* RORY.

RORY. What is aw this?

GOR. Have you a constable here?

RORY. Aye we have every thing snug and convenient among ourselves at Gretna Green.

GOR. Secure this fellow immediately.

RORY. He will come to be hang'd.

Lady PED. Well sir, (*to* Gorget.) since you have been so instrumental in securing me from infamy and destruction, I freely forgive you both—There children I wish you all happiness. (*joins their hands.*)

RORY. So there I shall have a job at last.

GOR.

Gor. Get off you scoundrel, and remember that tho' you escape justice this time, you are indebted for your life to this lady. (*Lady Ped.*)

Tip. Well now I have escap'd two great misfortunes in one day, the first hanging —and what was much greater by my soul, I have escap'd being married.

[*Exit.*

*Enter* Miss Plumb *and* Signiora.

Miss Plumb. Where is my husband?

Rory. Very near being hang'd lassie.

Maria. You have escap'd being united to a villain and a robber.

Miss Plumb. Then I'll return to town, and wait till I can get another lover.

Gor. Here will I seek for all my happiness. (*to* Maria.)

Gor. Secure in my Maria's heart,
    No longer shall we live asunder,
Tho' I yield to Cupid's dart,
    I always brav'd great Mars's Thunder,
Hymen Hymen god of marriage,
    To thee we drive in four-wheel'd carriage,
Thy temple's here on Gretna Green,
    O Hymen charming god of marriage.

Mar. With Gorget I at length am blest,
    A parent to our love consenting,
Thus be our passion still exprest,
    Still unembitter'd by repenting.
Hymen Hymen, &c.

L. Ped. Then Captain take Maria's hand,
    Be blest in wedlock's ties for ever;
Let virtue be your nuptial band,
    And folly ne'er your passion sever.
Hymen Hymen, &c.

Miss Pl. So smack to town in search of fun,
    And when I get a constant lover,

Again

GRETNA GREEN.

Again to Gretna Green I'll run,
  And all my prefent lofs recover,
Hymen, Hymen, &c.

SIG. Will no one run with me away?
  Will no one marry poor Signiora?
Since hufband I can't get to day
  I'll wed to-morrow and encora.
Hymen Hymen, &c.

RORY. Come ye young and come ye auld,
  Come ye rich and come ye needy
I'll chain ye for a purfe of gold,
  And fure ye cannot think me greedy!
Rory Rory the god of marriage,
  To me ye drive in foor-wheel'd carriage,
My temple's here on Gretna Green,
  Rory the blackfmith god of marriage.
Hymen Hymen, &c.

**F I N I S.**

Songs, Airs, etc. in the
Musical Farce Called Gretna Green

*Bibliographical note:*
*This facsimile has been made from a copy in the University Library, Cambridge England (M.R. 463.d.75.5[6])*

# SONGS, AIRS, &c.

### IN THE

## MUSICAL FARCE

#### CALLED

# GRETNA GREEN.

### AS PERFORMED AT THE

## THEATRE-ROYAL

#### IN THE

# HAY-MARKET.

---

## SECOND EDITION.

---

### LONDON:
Printed for T. CADELL, in the Strand.

M.DCC.LXXXIV.

# DRAMATIS PERSONÆ.

| | | |
|---|---|---|
| Captain Gorget, | - - | Mr. BANNISTER. |
| Rory, | - - - | Mr. WILSON. |
| Captain Tipperary, | - | Mr. EGAN. |

## WOMEN.

| | | |
|---|---|---|
| Lady Pedigree, | - - | Mrs. WEBB. |
| Maria, | - - - | Mrs. BANNISTER. |
| Miss Plumb, | - - | Miss MORRIS. |
| Signora Figurante, | - | Signora SESTINI. |

# SONGS, &c. &c.

## IN

# *GRETNA GREEN.*

---

## ACT I.

### AIR—*Rorer*

### *Dainty Davy.*

I Can fhoe a horfe, or kifs a lafs,
And nail twa lovers firm as brafs;
I can knock about the can and glafs
    In bumpers 'till I'm mellow!
Parents and guardians I defy,
Nay e'en the Court of Chancery;
The widow's tear, the virgin's figh,
    I ftop like a good fellow.

                    Auld

Auld maidens I deteſt,
Peeviſh, fretting,
Yet coquetting;
Batchelors can ne'er be bleſt;
Snarling and backbiting.
All ye fair wards! but come to me,
I'll grant ye Hymen's liberty;
To love and ſport with merry glee,
    As Mammy did before ye.

Then all ye bucks, and bloods, and beaux,
Bring each your girls, that are not foes
To wedding ſhoes, and wedding clothes,
    As Daddy did before ye!

    Auld maidens, &c.

---

### AIR II.—*Rory.*

#### *Paddy Whack.*

From fair London city they ſet out poſt flying,
And the Two Horns at Highgate they paſs in a
    crack;
      Cheek by jowl,
      My life, my ſoul,
      Day and night playing;

                  On

On dafhing,
Jades flafhing,
They fly at each fmack
Whip and fpur,
*Bur, bur, rur!*
All the-way fplafhing,
Driving and prancing,
And fpanking along!
Laughing and galloping,
Quaffing and walloping,
And fqueaking like two little pigs in a thong!

———

A I R  III.—*Signora.*

*French Air.*

Soft Arno's ftream how fweet, *divino!*
As on its flow'ry banks we rove!
Its cooling fhades, and neat *Cafino,*
Rural appear the feat of love.
There Tufcan youths, in foft *Soprano,*
Whifper the foothing amorous tale;
There Tufcan maids, in foft *piano,*
Coo, murm'ring with the fighing gale.

B                                        Oh,

Oh, lead me tó the calm *ripoſo*,
   Where all the loves and graces dwell;
Where every ſwain, *affetuoſo*,
   Tenderly ſighs his flame to tell!
Where every maid diſſolves in bliſſes,
   *Cara!* oh *Cara!* waft me there!
Where pains and ſorrows die in kiſſes,
   Kiſſes that charm, and heal deſpair!

---

## AIR IV.——*Rory.*

### *Jack o' Lanthern.*

My bottle is my wife and friend!
   If dull, her ſpirits rear me;
Whenever Rory would unbend,
   Oh how her kiſſes cheer me!

Lovely

Lovely bottle, warms my throttle,
  Makes me niddle-noddle queerly!
Stammer, ftumble, ftare, and tumble,
  Wimble, wamble, dearly.

## II.

She is my doctor and my nurfe,
  My champion in a hobble:
Altho' fhe empties oft my purfe,
  She makes my blood right noble.
      Lovely bottle, &c.

## III.

When by the middle I feize my wife,
  She fires me with love ftories:
As I'm wedded to her firm for life,
  I'll dance and fing her glories.
      Lovely bottle, &c.

AIR

## AIR V.——*Maria.*

*Etrick Banks.*

I dance, I laugh, I pipe, I fing,
  And merrily pafs the hours away :
The fleeting hours new bleffings bring,
  That keep me ever blithe and gay.
My food is hope, my drink is joy,
  My wealth a pure and lively mind ;
My happinefs knows no alloy,
  Unlefs when pity fays——" be kind!"

## AIR VI.——*Maria.*

### *Banks of the Tweed.*

My fond heart sweetly basks in the bright beams
  of hope;
Without it, those roses and lilies would drop:
'Tis the sun that illumes this parterre of true
  love;
Without hope I should droop, like the 'lorn
  turtle dove.
When my Jamie brav'd danger on Gibraltar's
  fell rock,
Hope kept off the balls, made my heart stand
  the shock!
And drew him return'd in all vict'ry's charms,
After conqu'ring his foes, to submit to these
  arms.

AIR

## AIR VII.——*Miſs Plumb.*

*Duraling.*

See gay Mrs. Toniſh, of Groſv'nor Place,
How charmingly ſhe enamels her face!
She pencils her veins with azure blue;
With black her eye-brows; combs them, too;
  She paints ſo true,
  In nature's hue,
With red and white, and Olympian dew,
As makes her look like a doll quite new,
And ſhoots Maccaronies thro' and thro'.

### II.

She drives ſo furious, hand in hand,
Tears up the pavement in the Strand;
Along Pall-mall ſo ſwiftly ſhe goes,
She ſcarce has time to nod at beaux.
  Up St. James's-ſtreet
  She gallops ſo fleet,
The bucks at Brookes's cannot greet her;
For ere from play they can move their feet,
She's giving the go-by down next ſtreet.

F I-

# FINALE.

By *Rory, Signora, Maria,* and Miſs *Plumb.*

*Low down in the Broom.*

## RORY.

Blind Cupid's darts ſtrike every man,
  At random tho' they fly;
From ſparkling glaſs and jolly can,
  They ſhoot and blind----my eye!
What brightens nature's darkeſt nights,
  But love, that beauteous boy!
The moon is Hymen's torch that lights
  Each loving pair to joy!

## MARIA.

Impatient----I for Thyrſis wait,
  And at his bleſt return
He'll find his tender conſtant mate
  With pureſt paſſion burn.
           What brightens, &c.

*Miſs*

#### M.rs Plumb.

Then I to London fhall return;
  For tho' not yet fixteen,
I'll danger for a hufband fpurn,
  And drive to Gretna Green.
                What brightens, &c:

#### Signora.

And I to Opera will repair;
  For that's the charming fpot
Where Veftris danc'd with heavenly air,
  Seftini thrill'd her note!
                What brightens, &c:

#### End of the FIRST ACT:

ACT

# A C T  II.

## A I R  I.—*Rory.*

### *Country Bumpkin.*

I Saw a ſtout fellow ride very queer,
  *Hotchity, botchity, ſhakity, quakity!*
The drops run down his faee with fear,
  And the mane he held for the bridle.
To keep him faſt on, he put ſpurs in its ſides,
  *Kickity, ſtickity, friſkity, whiſkity!*
The ſaddle ſlipp'd round, and he ſtuck to the
    hide;
  And d'ye think, my good folks, he was idle?

### II.

He rode not along, but acroſs the highway,
  *Stumblety, tumblety, hitchity, ditchity!*
Oh, what a good ſoul! for his prayers he did ſay,
  When on the ground he lay bawling.
                C                    I quickly

I quickly to his relief bent my courfe,
*Runnity, funnity, gigglety, nigglety!*
How I laugh'd when I faw neither man nor horfe,
But a mare, and a tailor, a fprawling!

———————

**A I R  II.—***Lady Pedigree.*

*Sweet Richard, a Welch tune.*

Soon as a forward girl is grown
To fixteen years of age,
Our daughter is no more our own,
A lover's all her rage.
A handfome fhape, a pleafing air,
Red coat, and fmart cockade,
Big looks, Small talk, confpire to bear
To Gretna Green, the jade.

A I R

## AIR III.——*Signora.*

### *Giordani.*

Away, you wild, inconſtant lover,
  You'll never win me by your wiles!
All your deceit I now diſcover,
  The faithleſs vow and look beguiles.
Since I find that you're a rover,
  In vain are roguiſh arts and ſmiles.

———————

## AIR IV.——*Maria.*

### *Logan Water.*

Since that dear day my heart you gain'd;
  On the wild thyme bank where vi'lęts blow,
For you alone this throat has ſtrain'd,
  For you alone this breaſt could glow.
How often have I penſive ſtray'd,
  To the tree where you engrav'd my name!
And when I ſaw each letter fade,
  I cry'd, " You had fallen a prey to fame!"

**AIR**

AIR  V.—*Captain Gorget.*


*Flowers of Edinburgh.*


With honour's fcars
Retir'd from the wars,
The veteran is a noble fight:
His ftains are all
By fword and ball,
Thofe crimfon badges of his might!
His tales infpire
Heroic fire,
To ev'ry youthful breaft around:
With valour's ftrong fhield,
For their King they take the field,
And retire in old age, full of glory crown'd!

### AIR VI.—*Captain Gorget.*

### Dr. ARNOLD.

September the thirteenth, proud Bourbon may
    mourn;
  Elliot's lightnings and thunders,
  Like Jove's bolts, did wonders!
    With shot red hot
    Don Moreno was torn,
On the hills the spectators with grief rend the
    sky.
  Their ships are all on fire:
  Hark! what shrieks! some expire,
    Up they blow,
    Up they blow,
  And thousands now go
  To the bottom low, low, low.
Whilst wreck'd hundreds despairing for safety
    loud cry;
    For safety out cry,
    For safety out cry,
And they find it in Curtis's humanity.

AIR VII.——*Signora.*

*Giordani.*

From branch to branch the feather'd pair
  Fly chirping fweet the pleafing ftrain;
The cares of love their only care,
  And paffion fooths their heart felt pain.
Hark! liften to the nightingale,
  Whofe mellow notes falute the fpring!
On yonder fpray fhe loves to wail,
  And tenderly, tho' fadly, fing!

F I-

# FINALE.

*Old Highland Laddie.*

### Captain GORGET.

Secure in my Maria's heart,
  No longer fhall we live afunder!
Tho' I yield to Cupid's dart,
  I always brav'd great Mars's thunder!
Hymen, Hymen, God of Marriage!
  To thee we drive in four-wheel carriage:
Thy temple's here on Gretna Green,
  Hymen, the charming God of Marriage!

### MARIA.

With Gorget I at length am bleft,
  A parent to our love confenting;
Thus be our paffion ftill expreft,
  Still unembitter'd by repenting!

### Lady PEDIGREE.

Then, Captain, take Maria's hand,
  Be bleft in wedlock's ties for ever!
Let virtue be your nuptial band,
  And folly ne'er your paffion fever!
Hymen, Hymen, &c.

*Mifs*

( 24 )

*Miſs* PLUMB.

So ſmack to town, in ſearch of fun!
And when I get a conſtant lover,
Again to Gretna Green I'll run,
And all my preſent loſs recover.

SIGNORA.

Will no one run with me away?
Will no one marry poor Signora?
Since huſband I can't get to-day,
I'll wed to-morrow---and *Ancora.*

CHORUS.

Hymen, Hymen, &c.

THE END.